GABI WOLF

MiniMania

❖ COLORING BOOK ❖

3

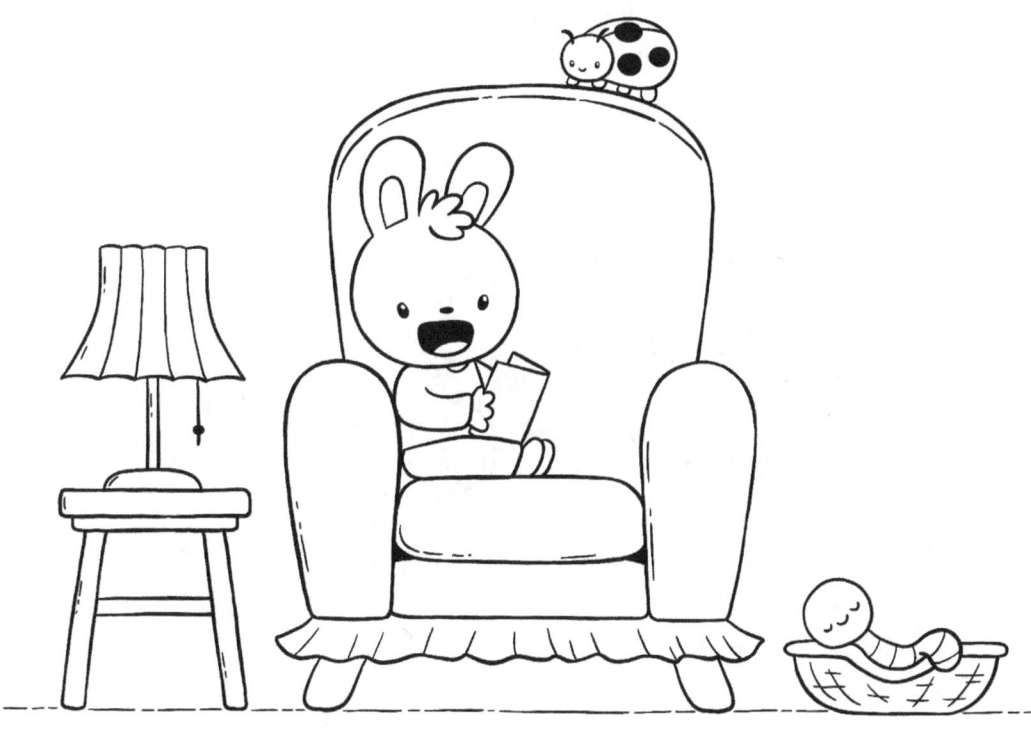

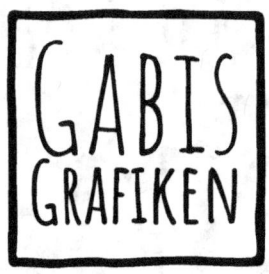

ISBN: 979-8876200501
Independently published
Cover & Illustrations: Gabi Wolf

This book
belongs to:

_____

_____

_____

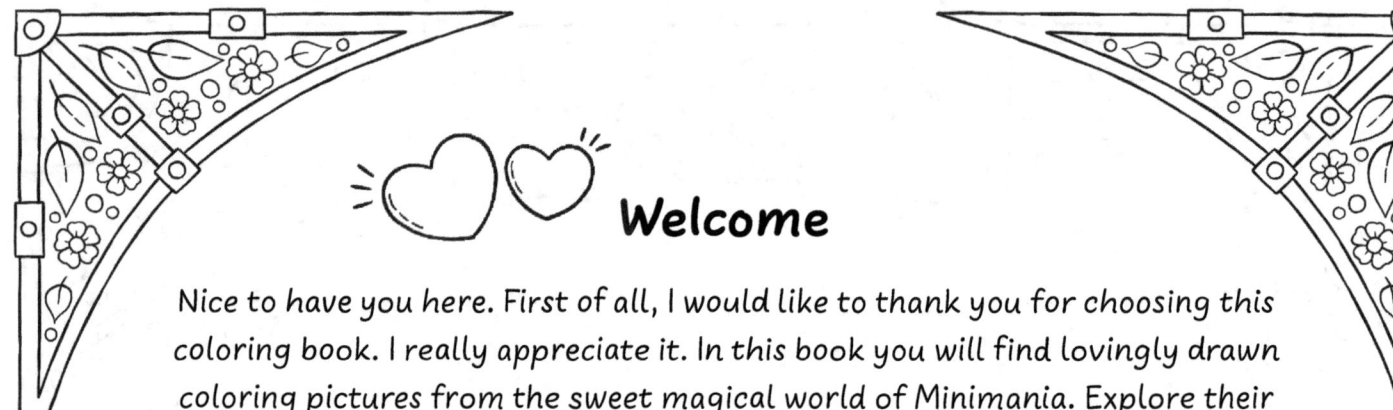

Welcome

Nice to have you here. First of all, I would like to thank you for choosing this coloring book. I really appreciate it. In this book you will find lovingly drawn coloring pictures from the sweet magical world of Minimania. Explore their secret worlds and bring them to life through color.

To make sure you have fun coloring, I recommend placing a few sheets of paper under the picture you're working on. This is a good base and prevents the color from pressing through or transferring to the page underneath.

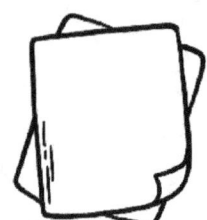

This book is not designed like most others coloring books, but is divided into two sections. In both parts you will find coloring pictures, but the color of the outline is different.

Part 1

The first part is a classic coloring book and is intended for all those who simply want to color in a relaxed way. Each picture has black outlines and the white areas can be colored in as usual. You don't have to worry and can get started straight away.

This first part can also be used to experiment with colors or techniques. If you don't like a color combination, you can paint the picture again using colors in the second part. Or you can paint with markers in the first part and with colored pencils in the second.

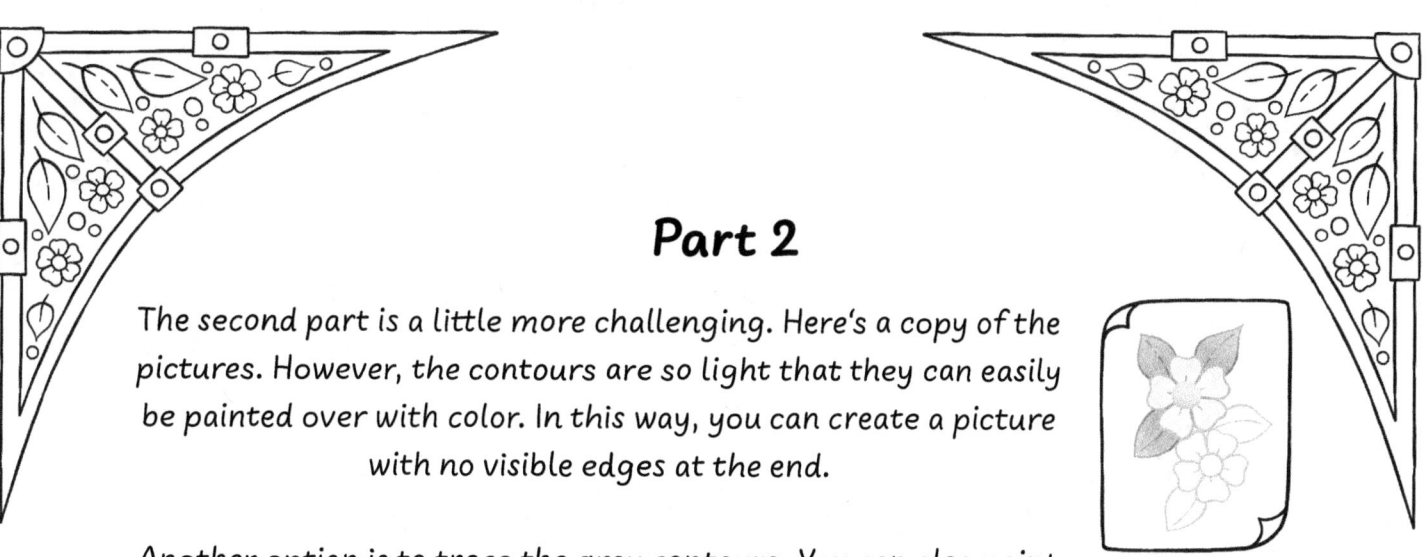

Part 2

The second part is a little more challenging. Here's a copy of the pictures. However, the contours are so light that they can easily be painted over with color. In this way, you can create a picture with no visible edges at the end.

Another option is to trace the gray contours. You can also paint your own ideas such as flowers or characters into the white areas. However, the lines don't have to be black. Brown or dark blue lines also look nice and purple lines go perfectly with a pastel-colored background.

No matter which option you choose, in the end you will have created your own personal work of art and I would be delighted if you shared it on social media. Please use #gabisgrafiken or @gabiwolf so that I can find your picture.

I'm also always happy to receive feedback on my books. This helps me make the next books even more varied and interesting. You can contact me via Instagram, Facebook, YouTube or email. I promise to reply to every message. Of course, I'm also happy to receive a review on Amazon.

And now I wish you lots of fun coloring.

www.gabiwolf.de
hello@gabiwolf.de

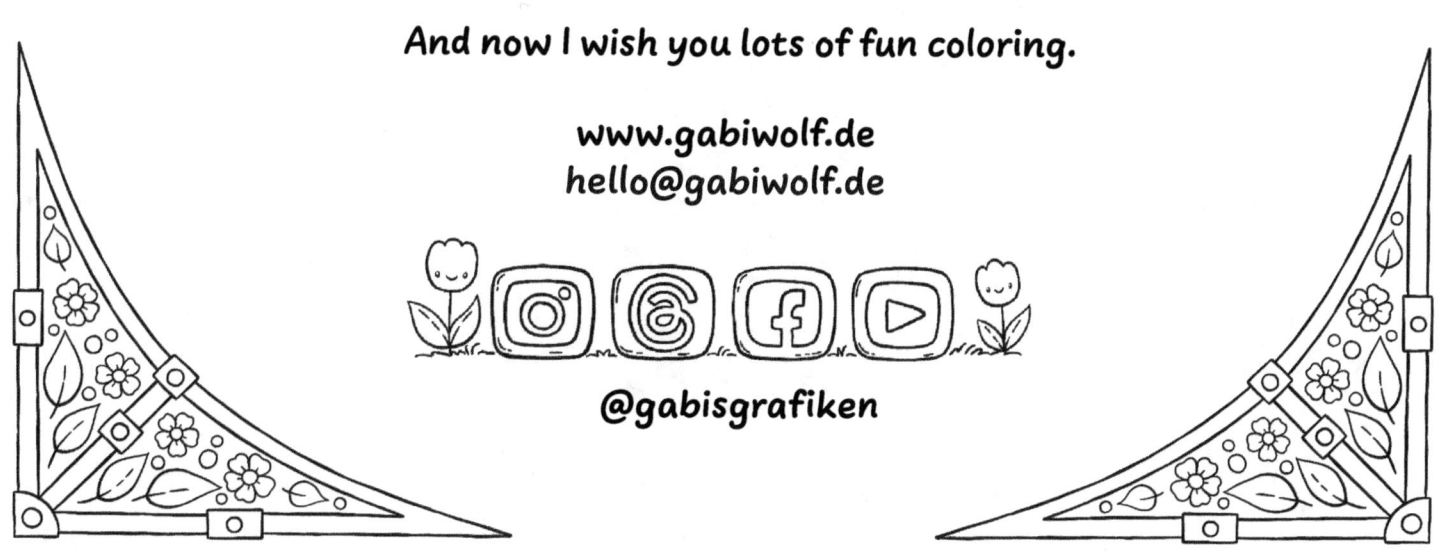

@gabisgrafiken

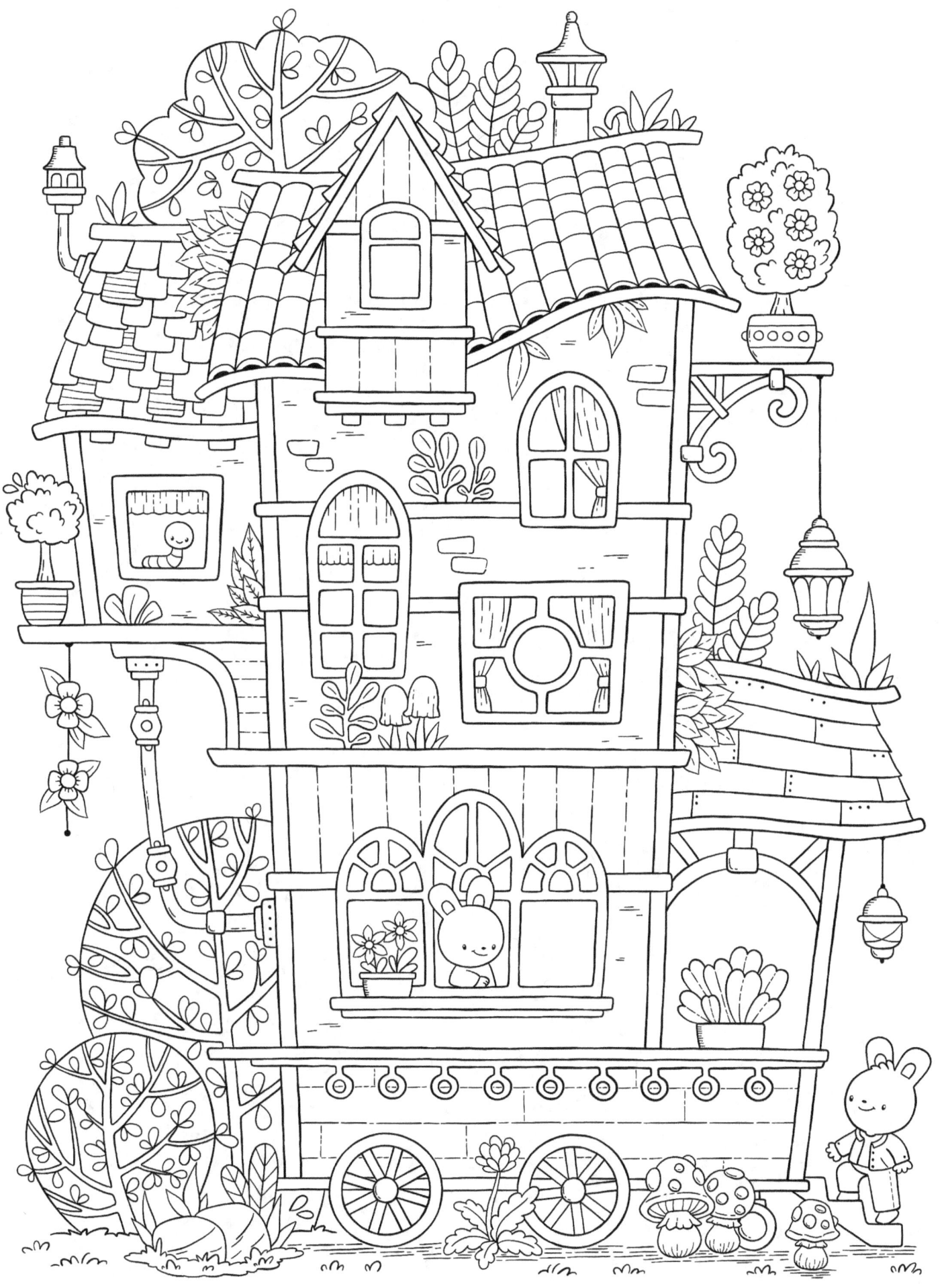

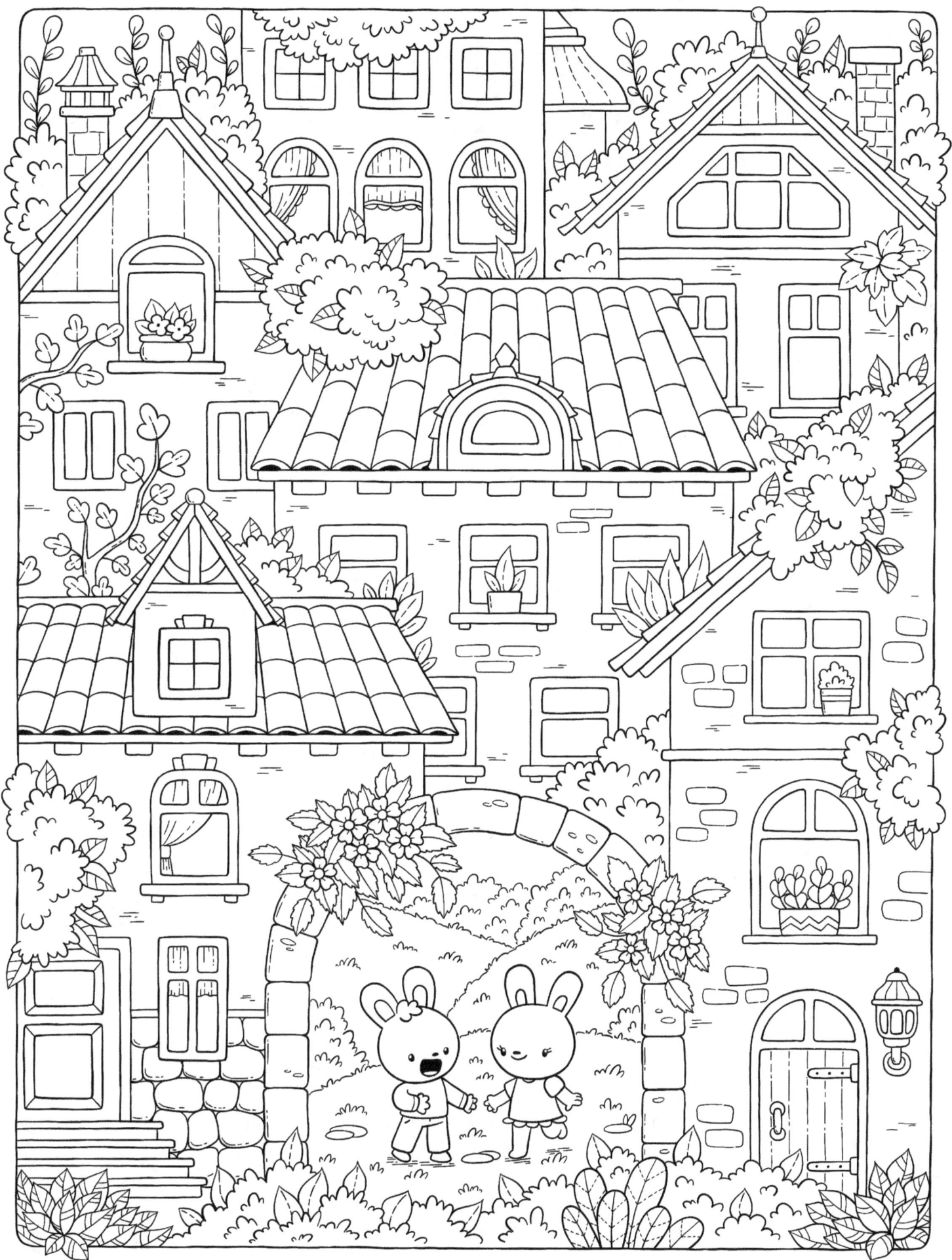

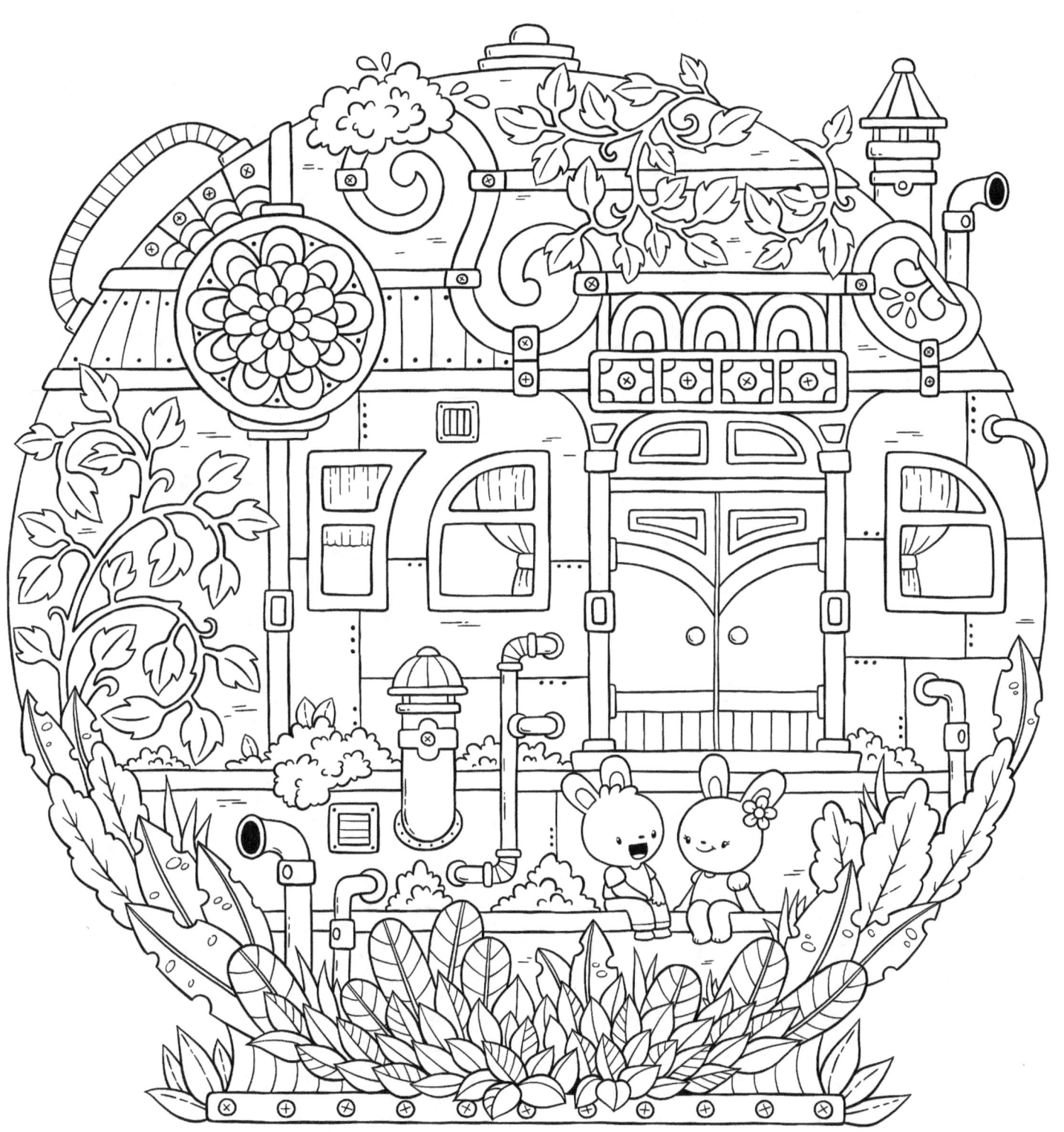

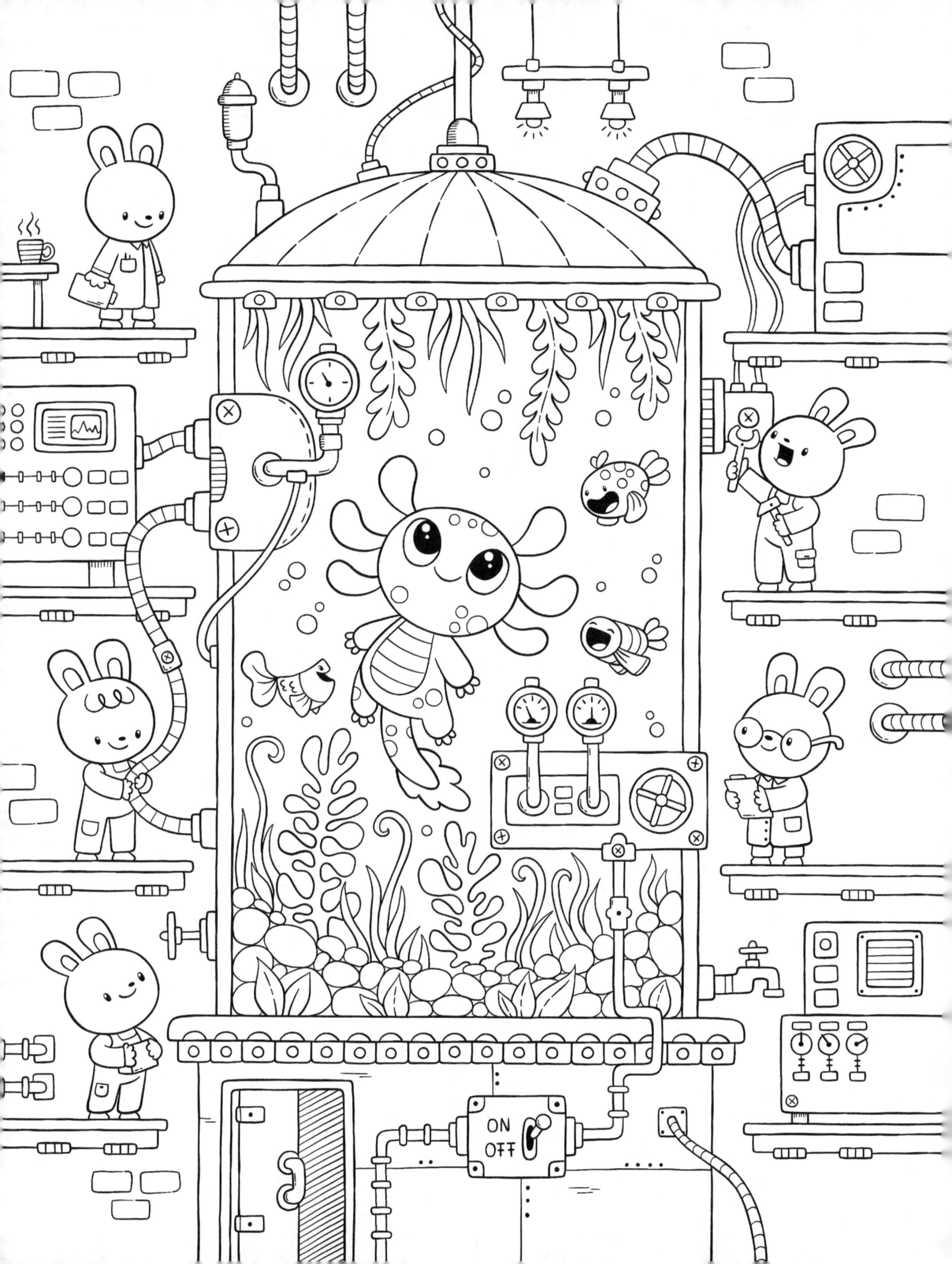

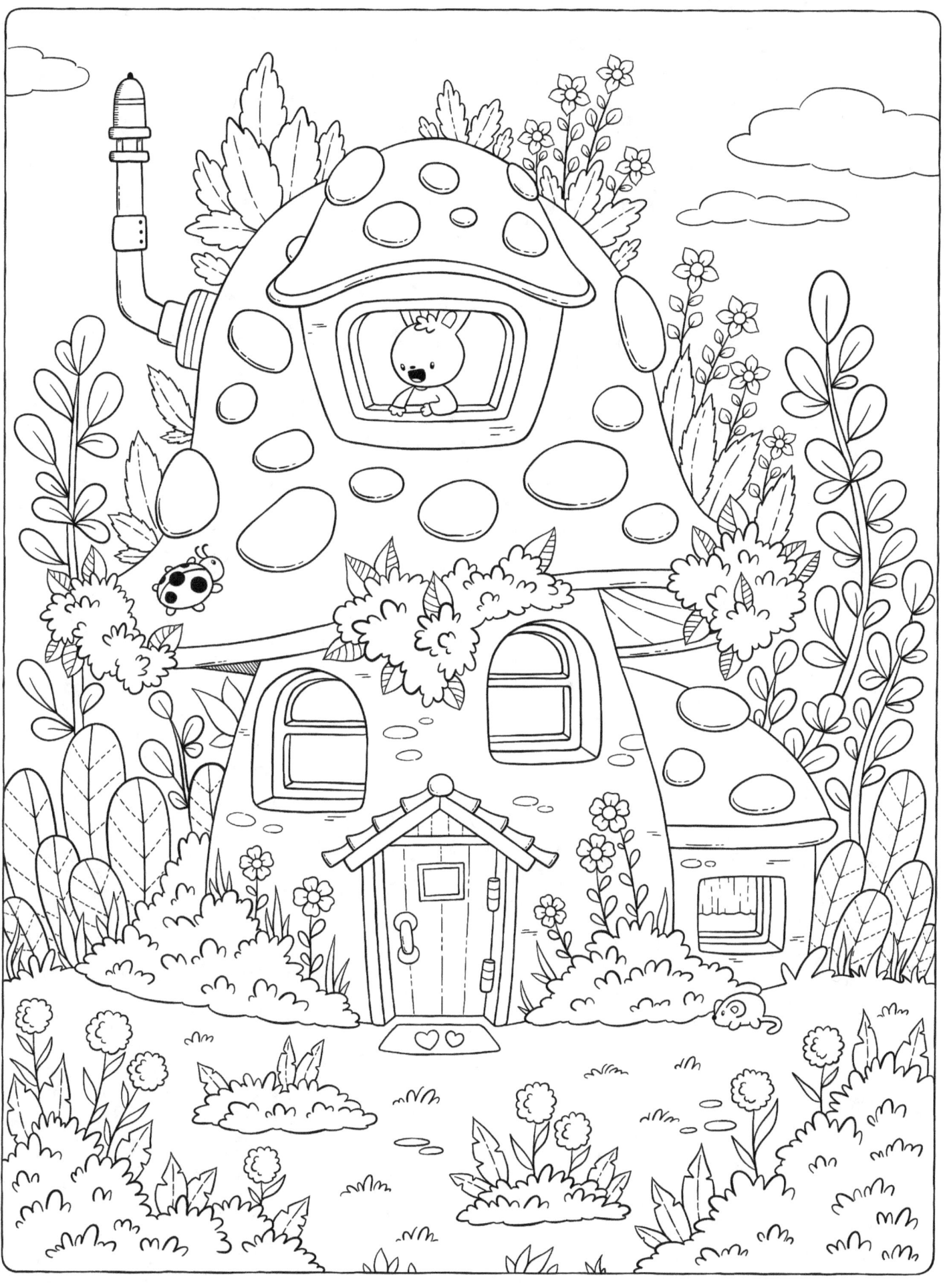

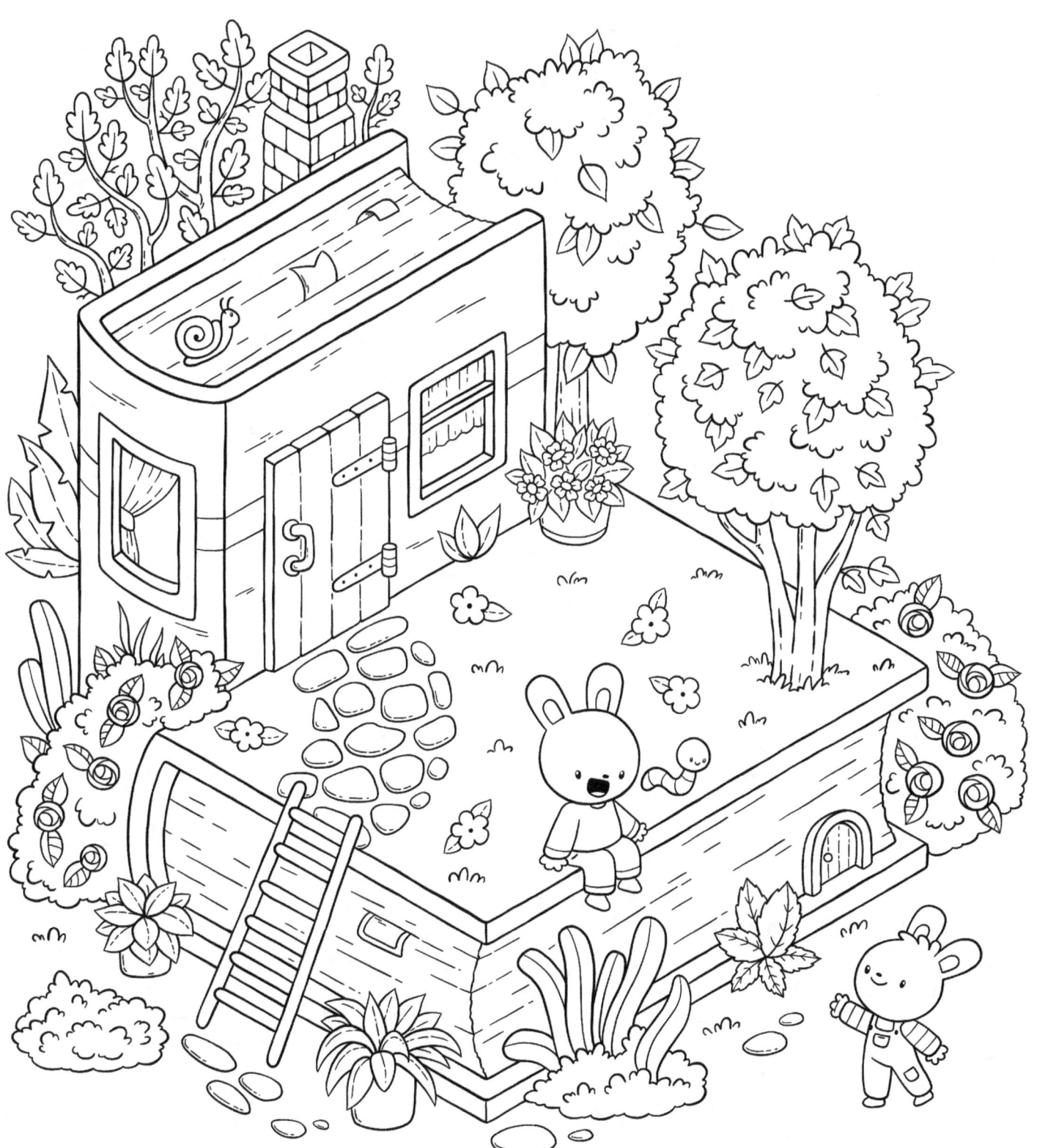

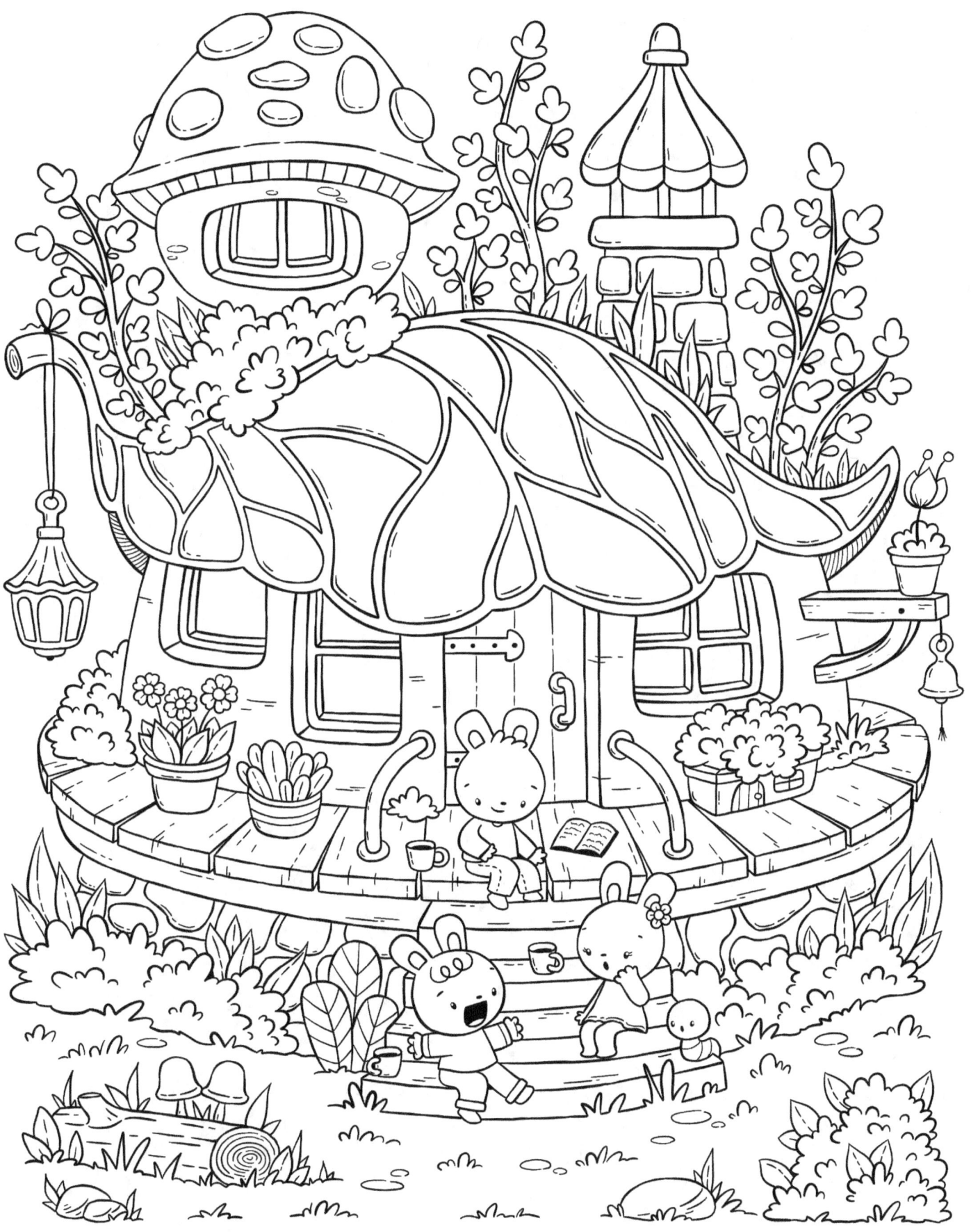

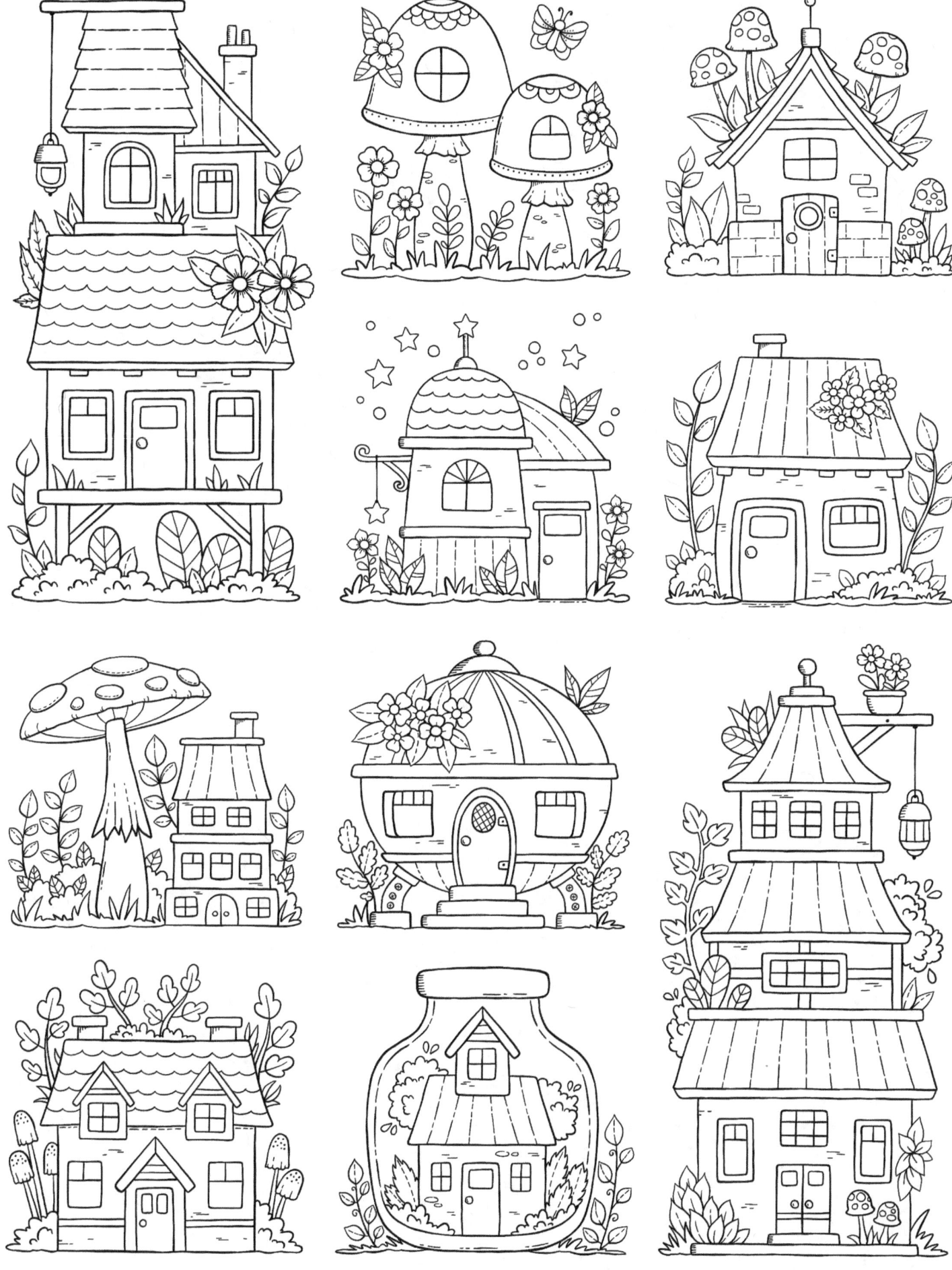

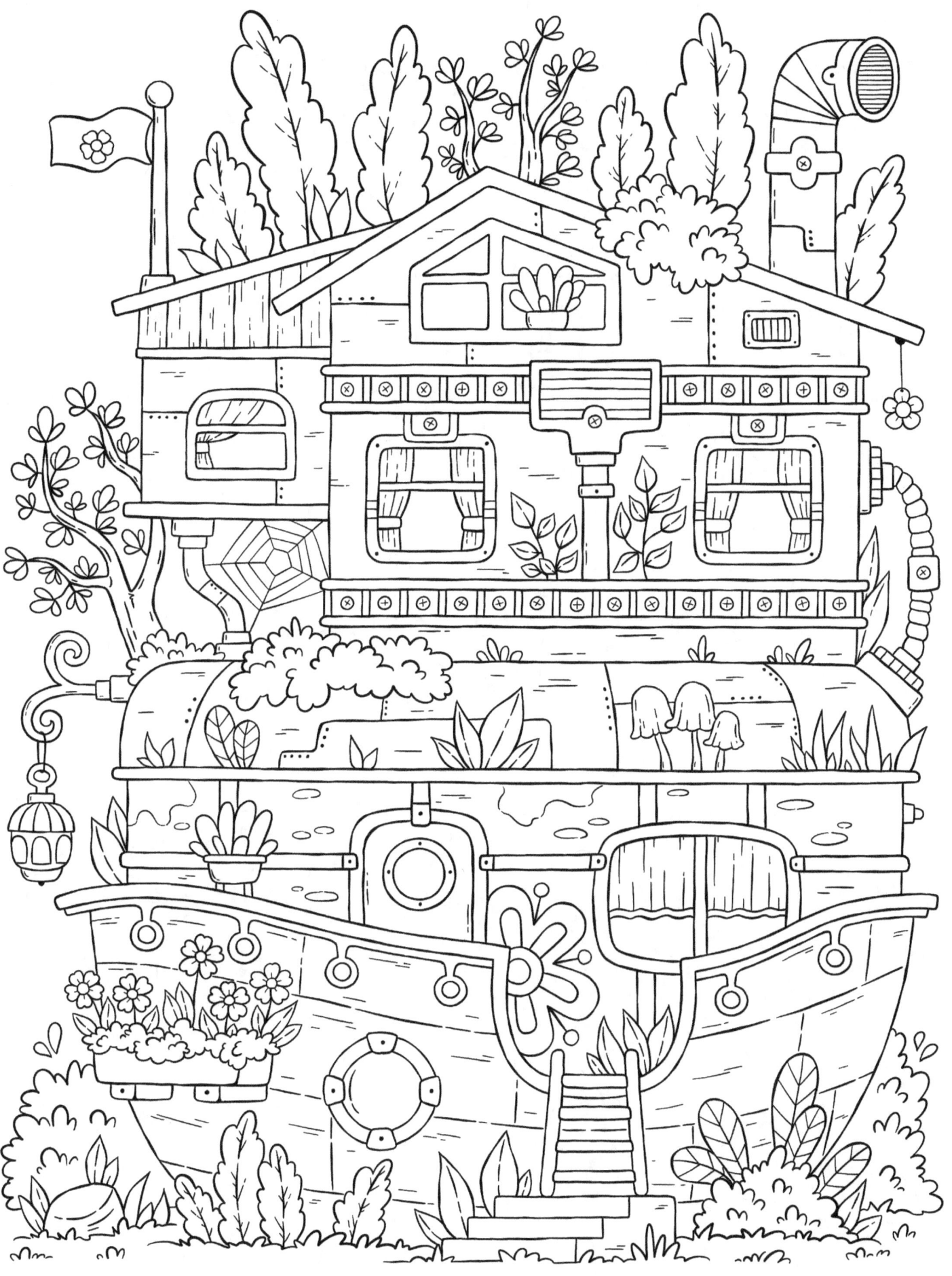

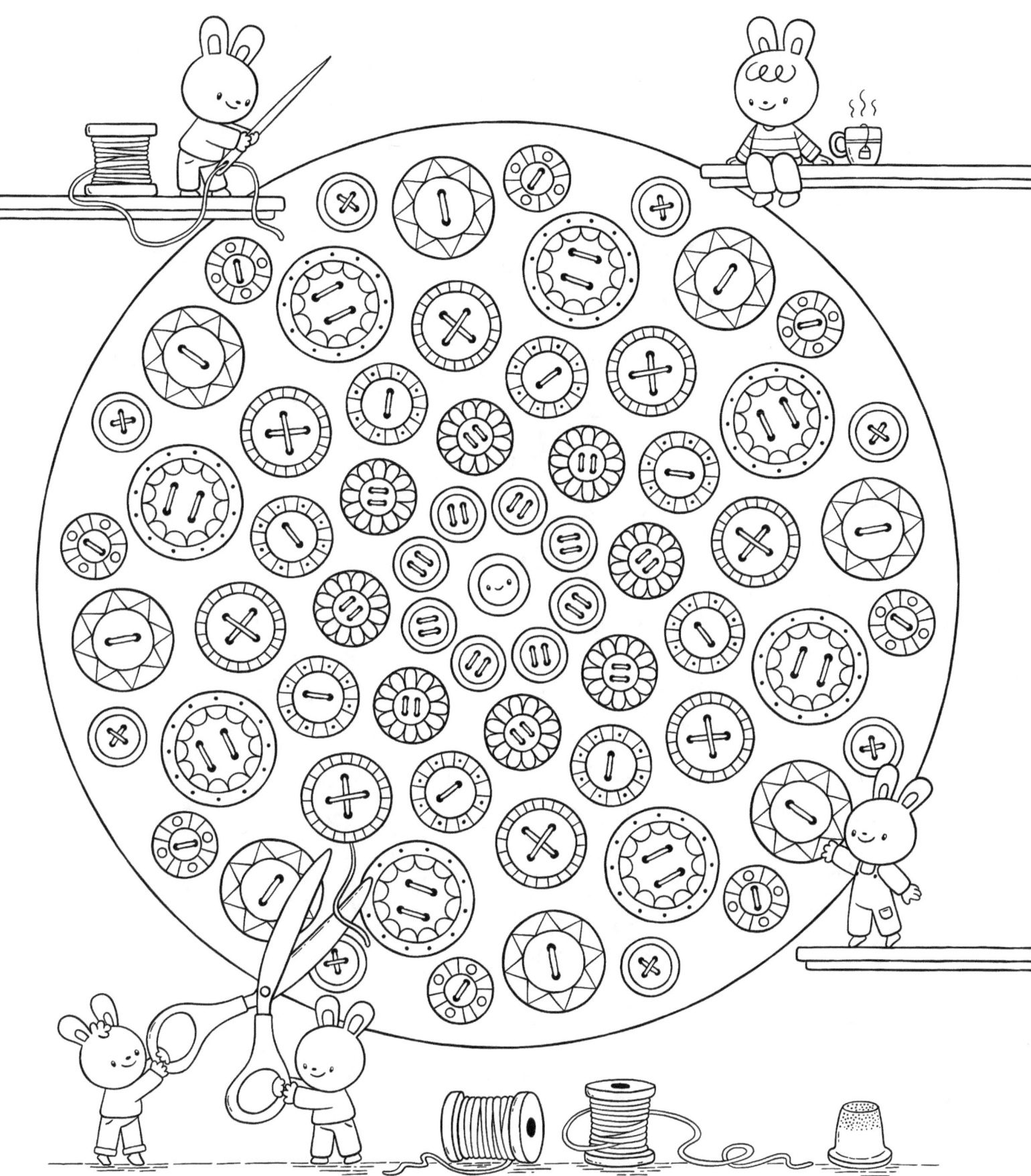

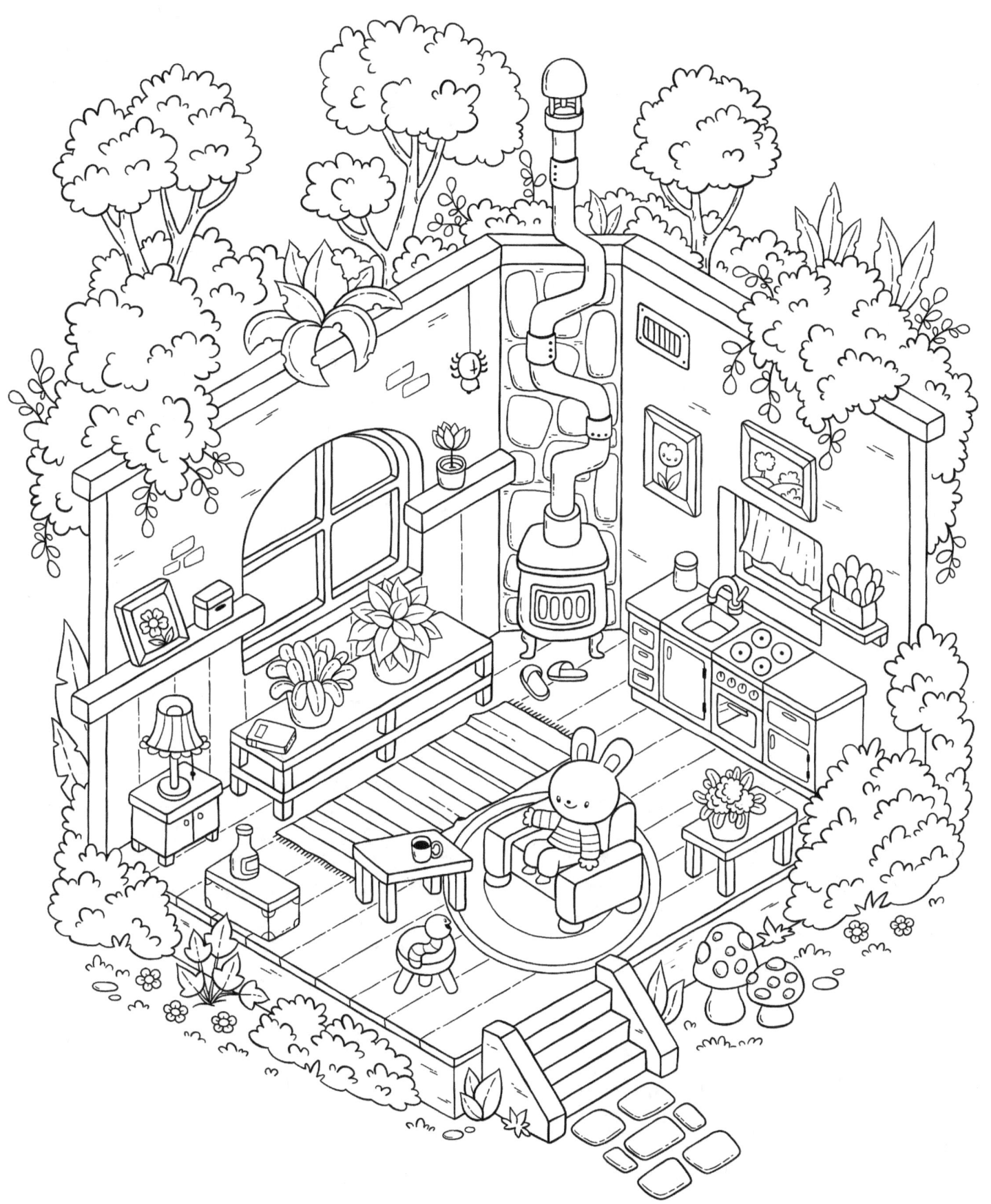

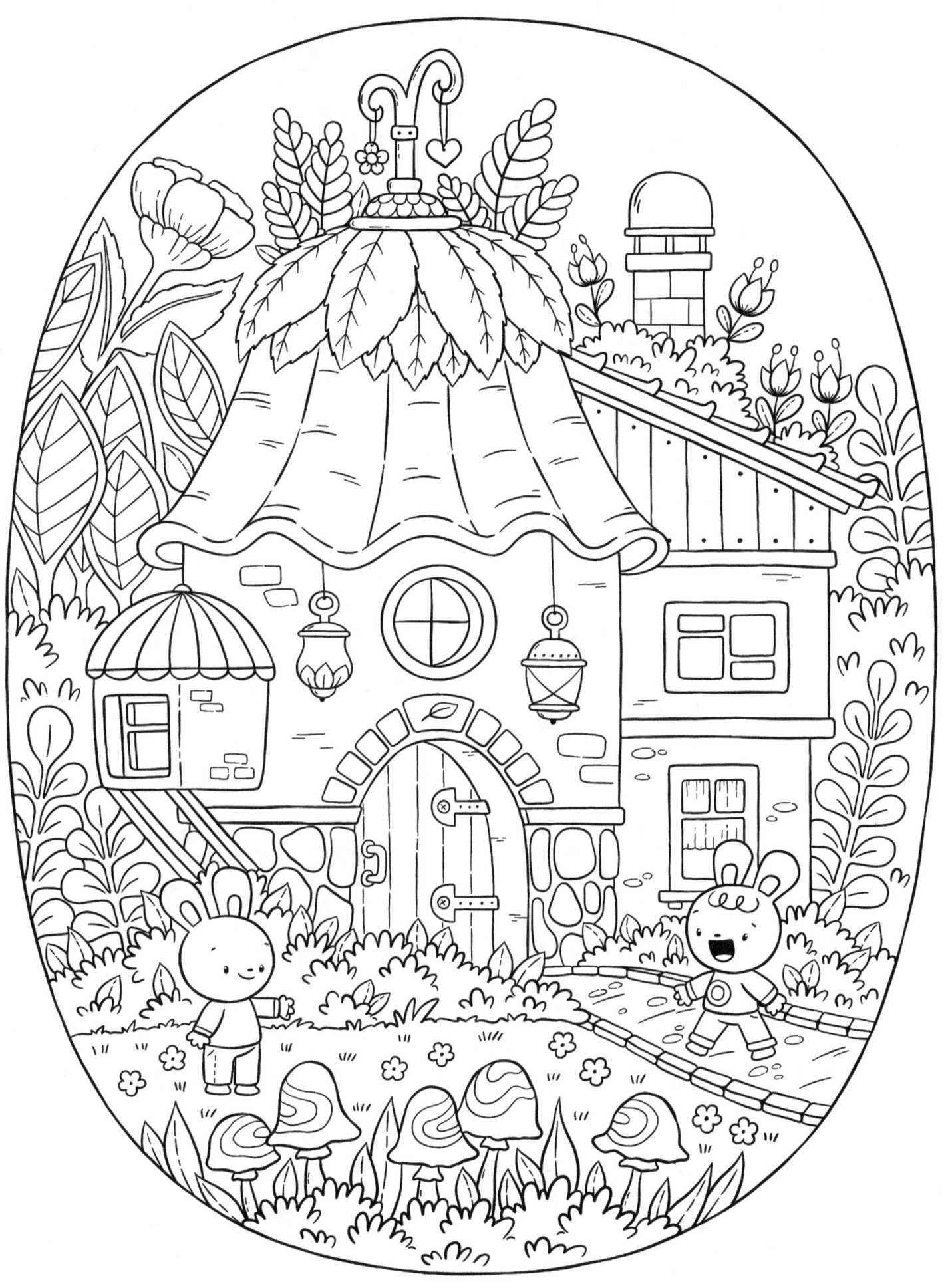

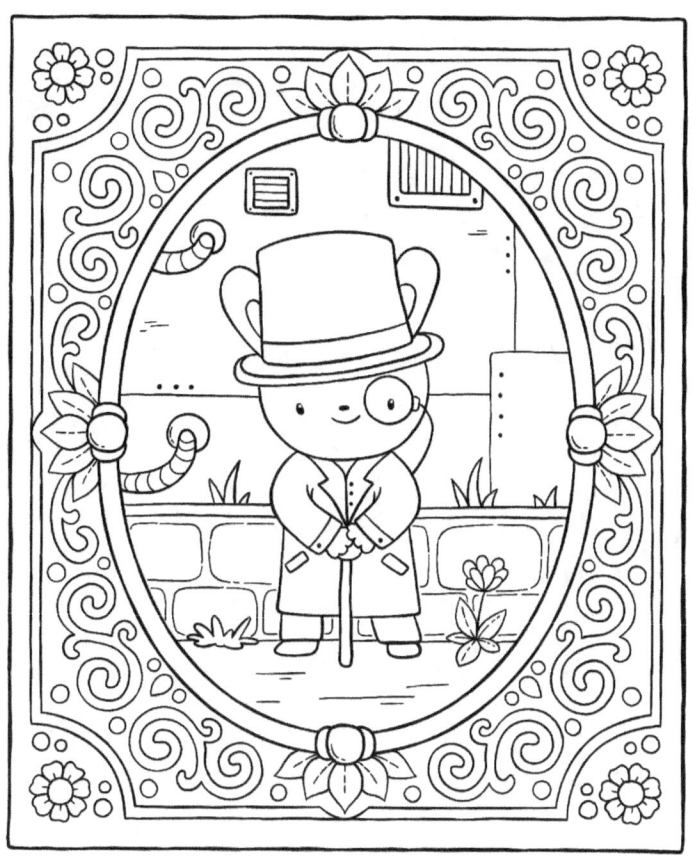
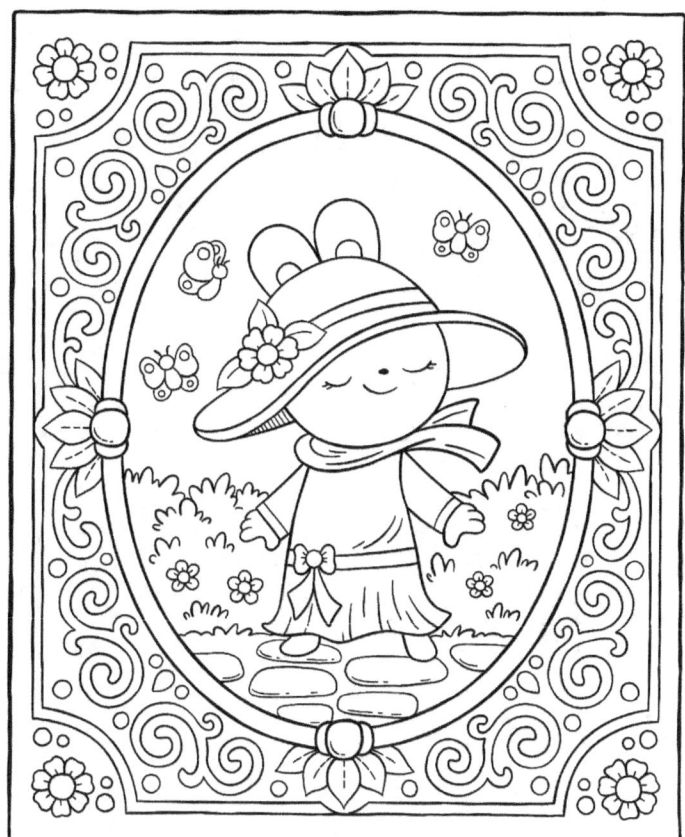
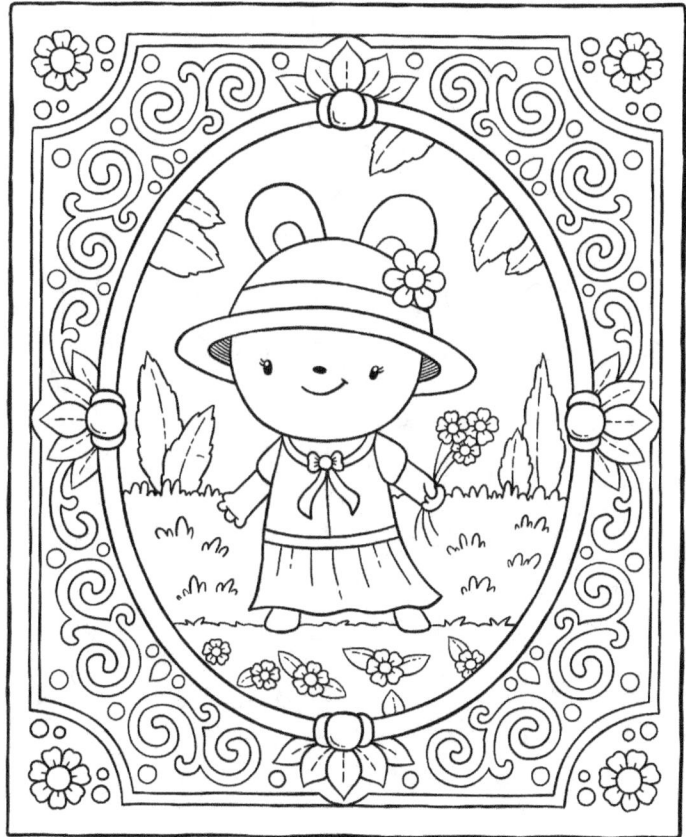
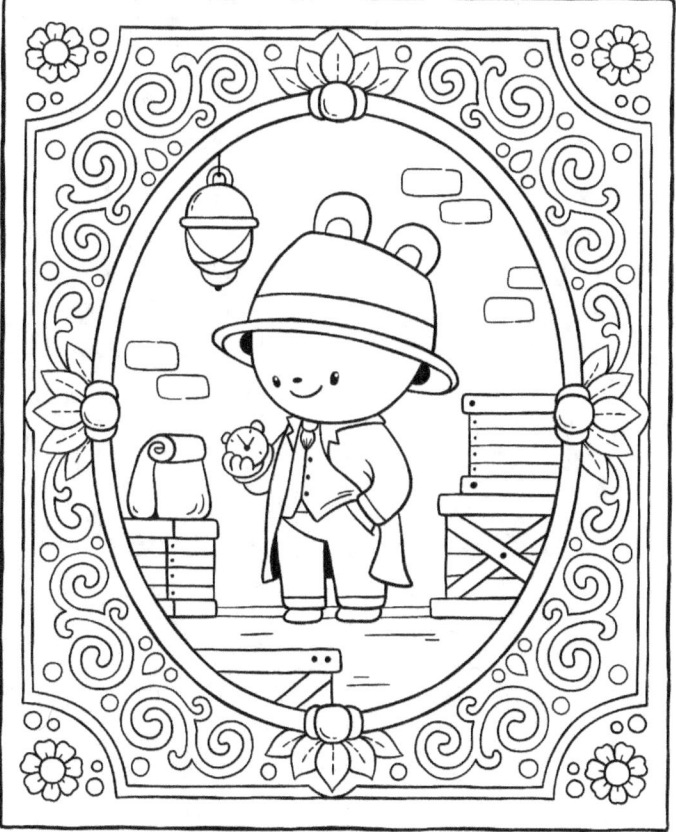

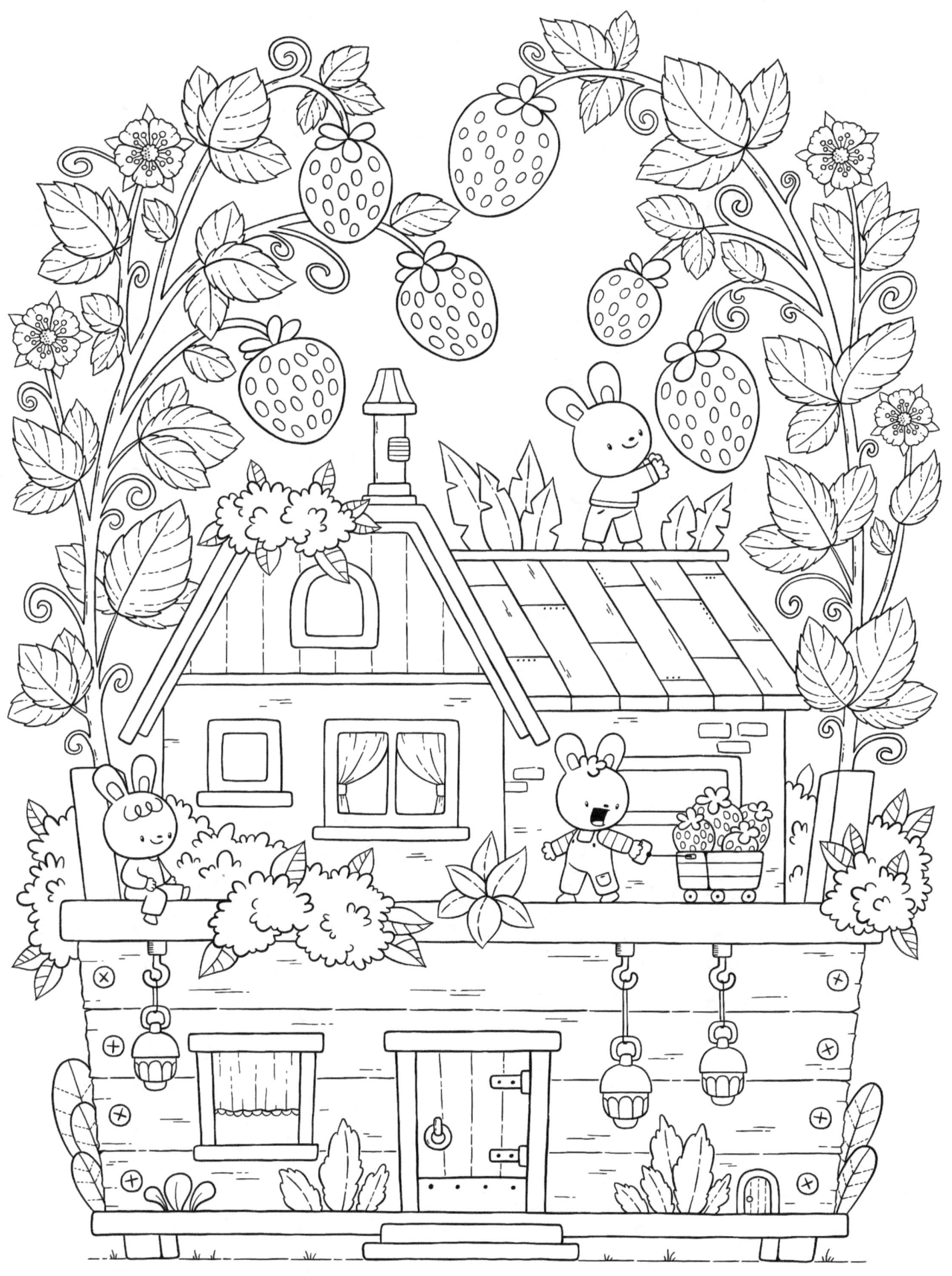

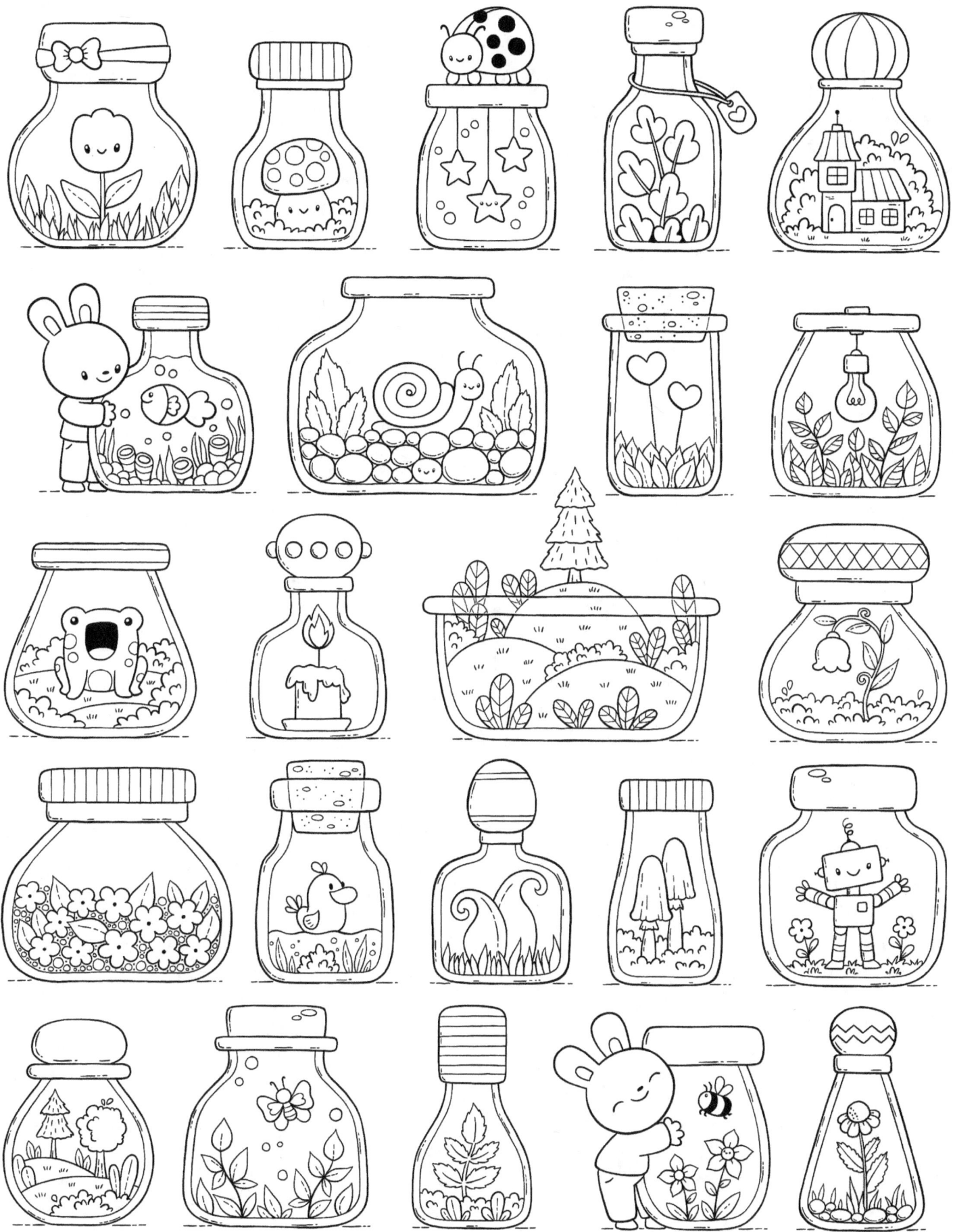

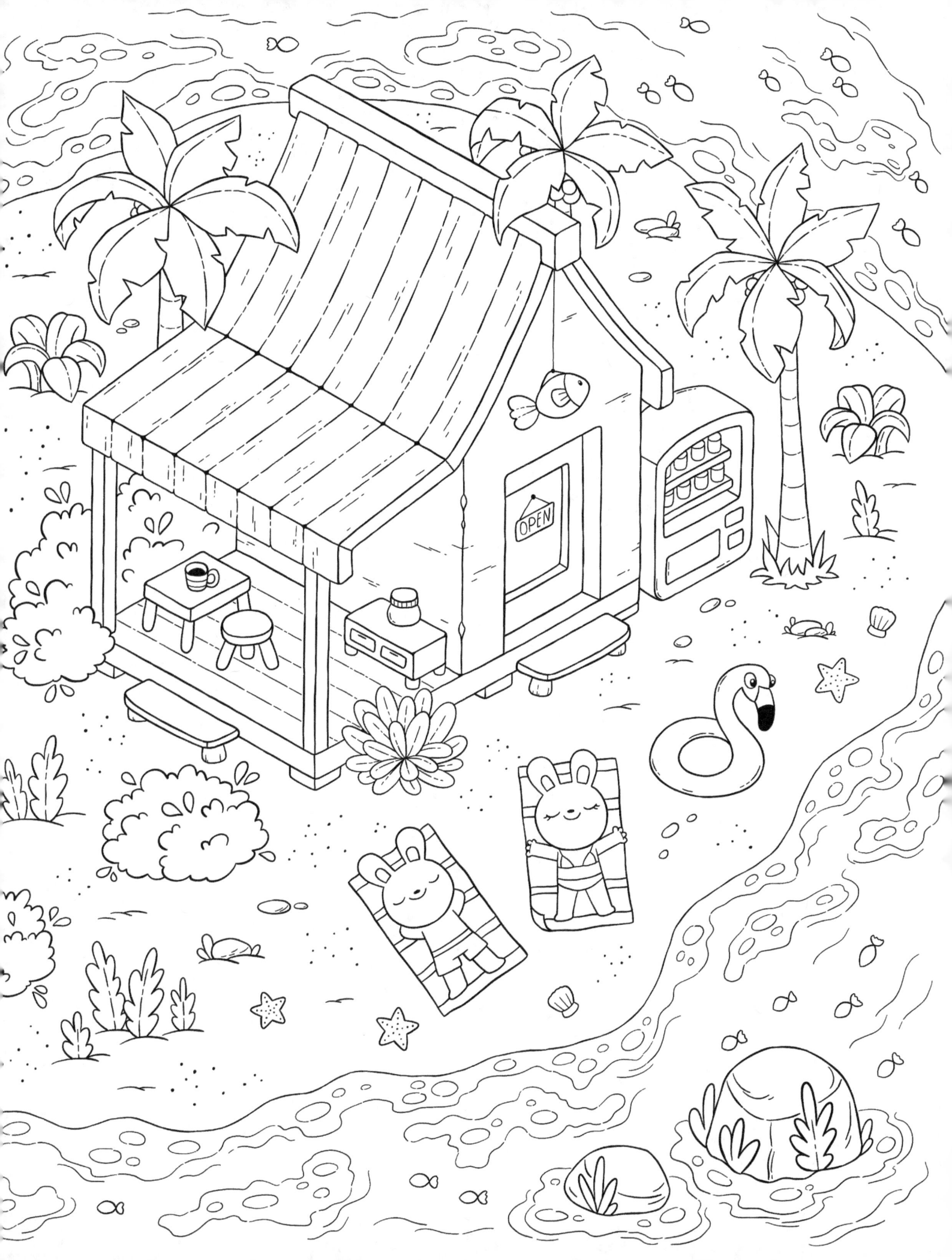

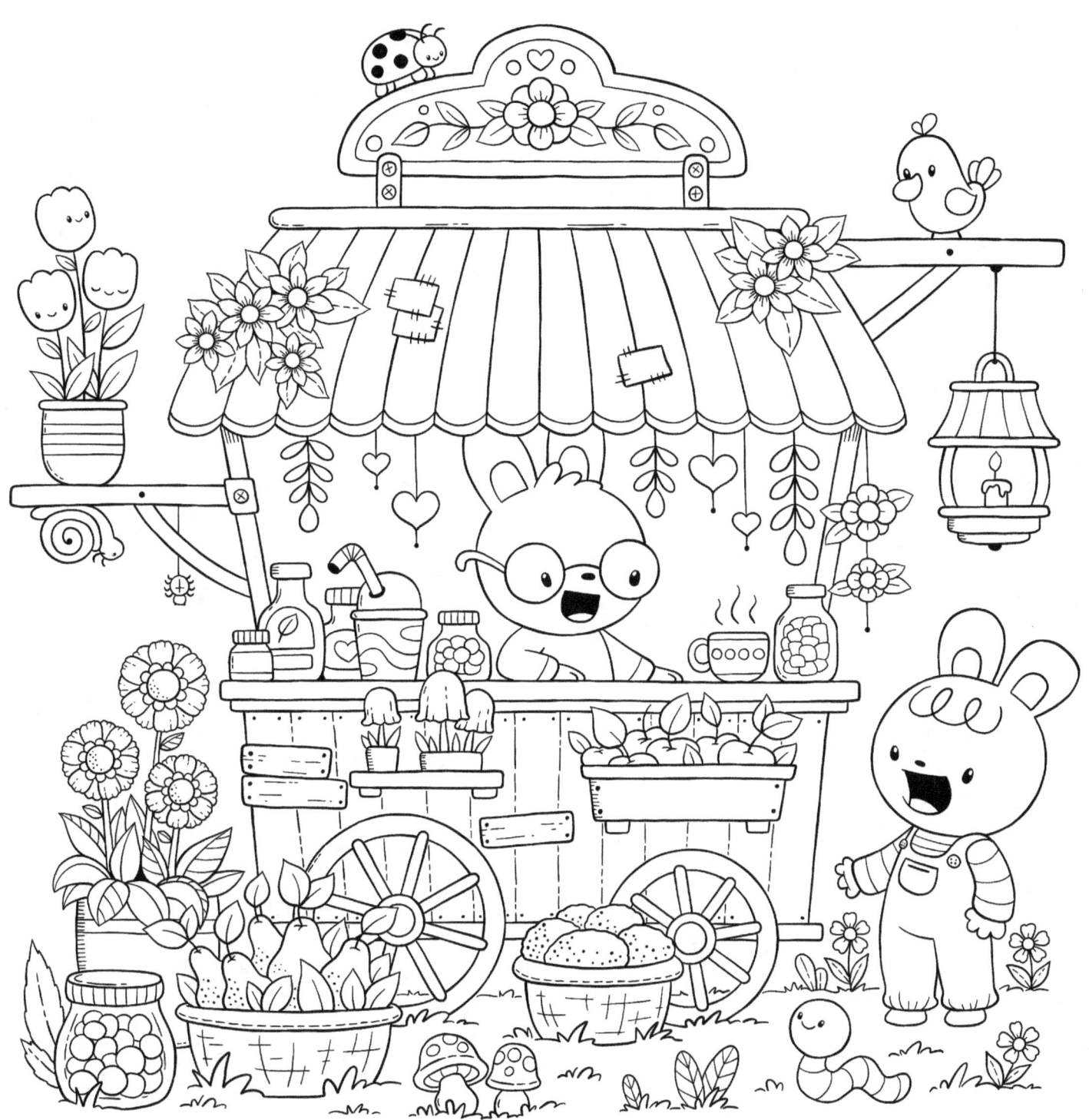

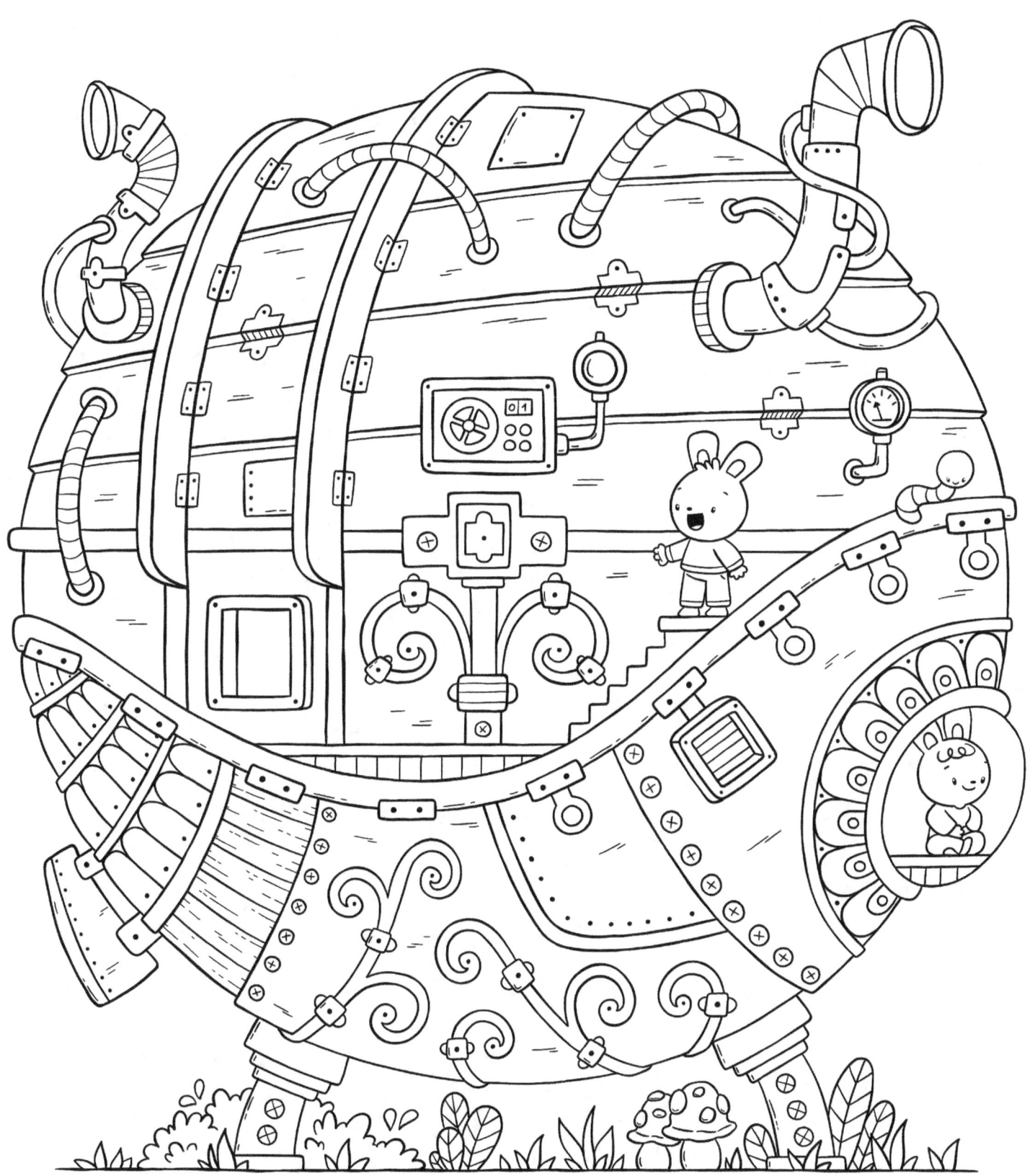

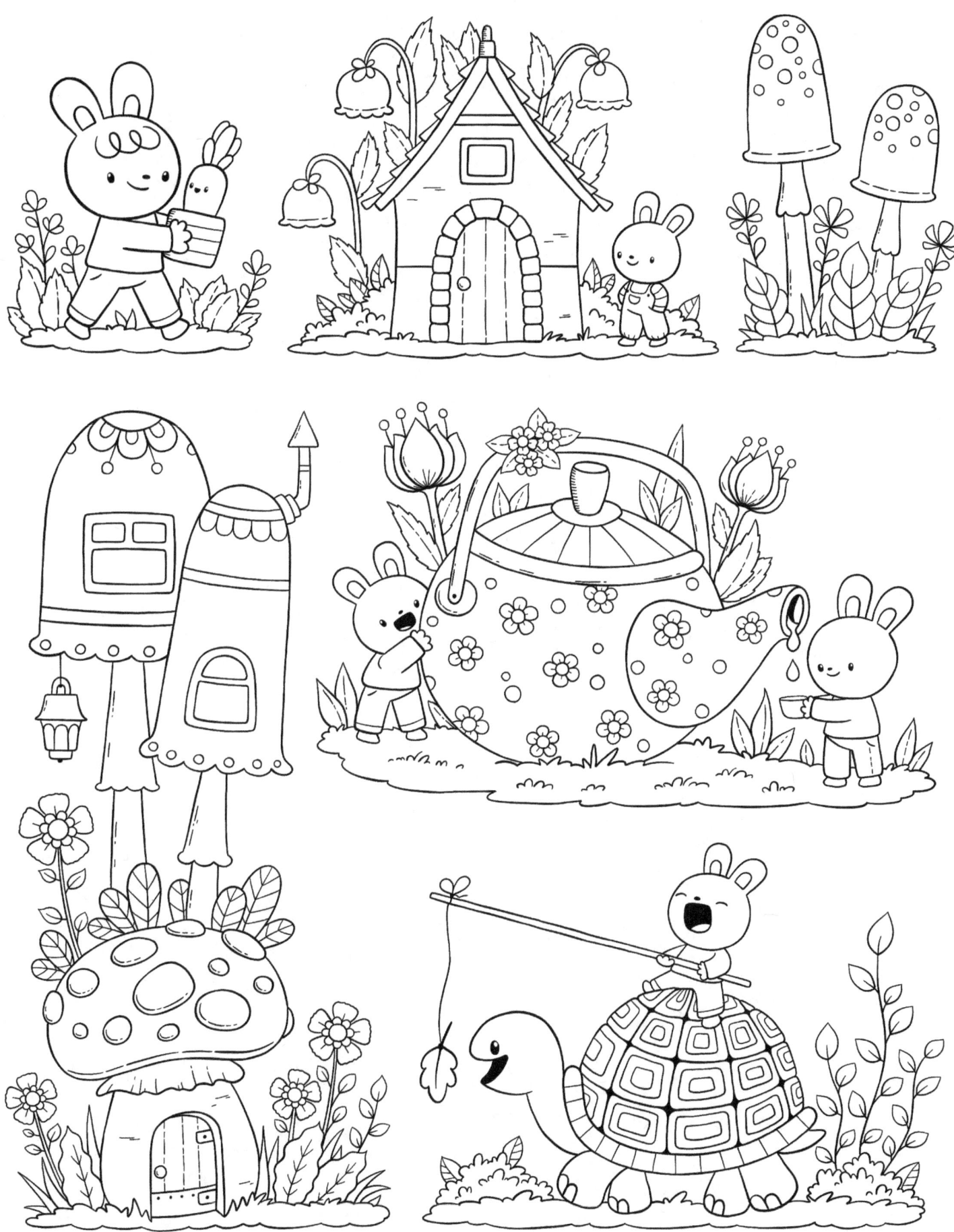

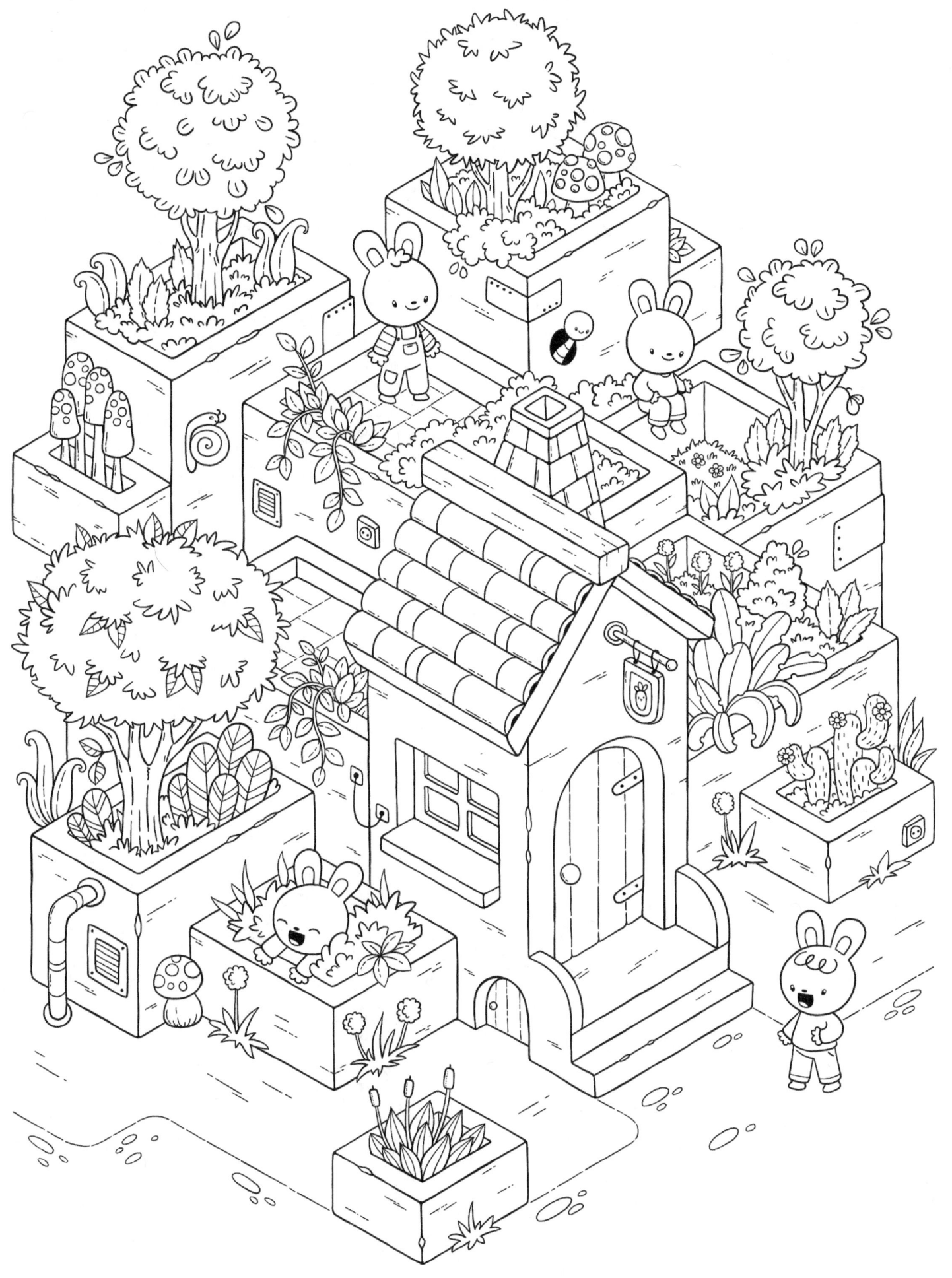

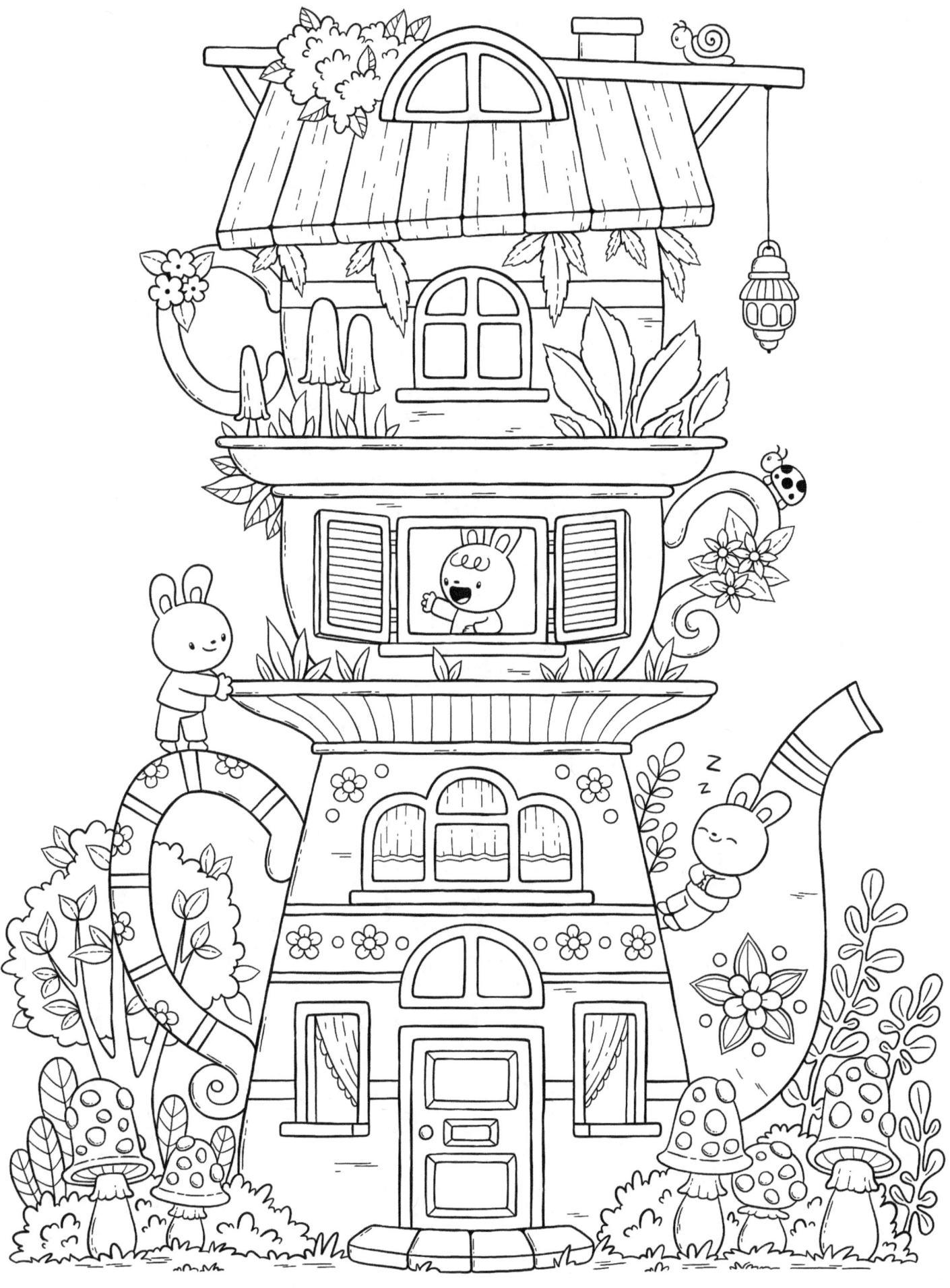

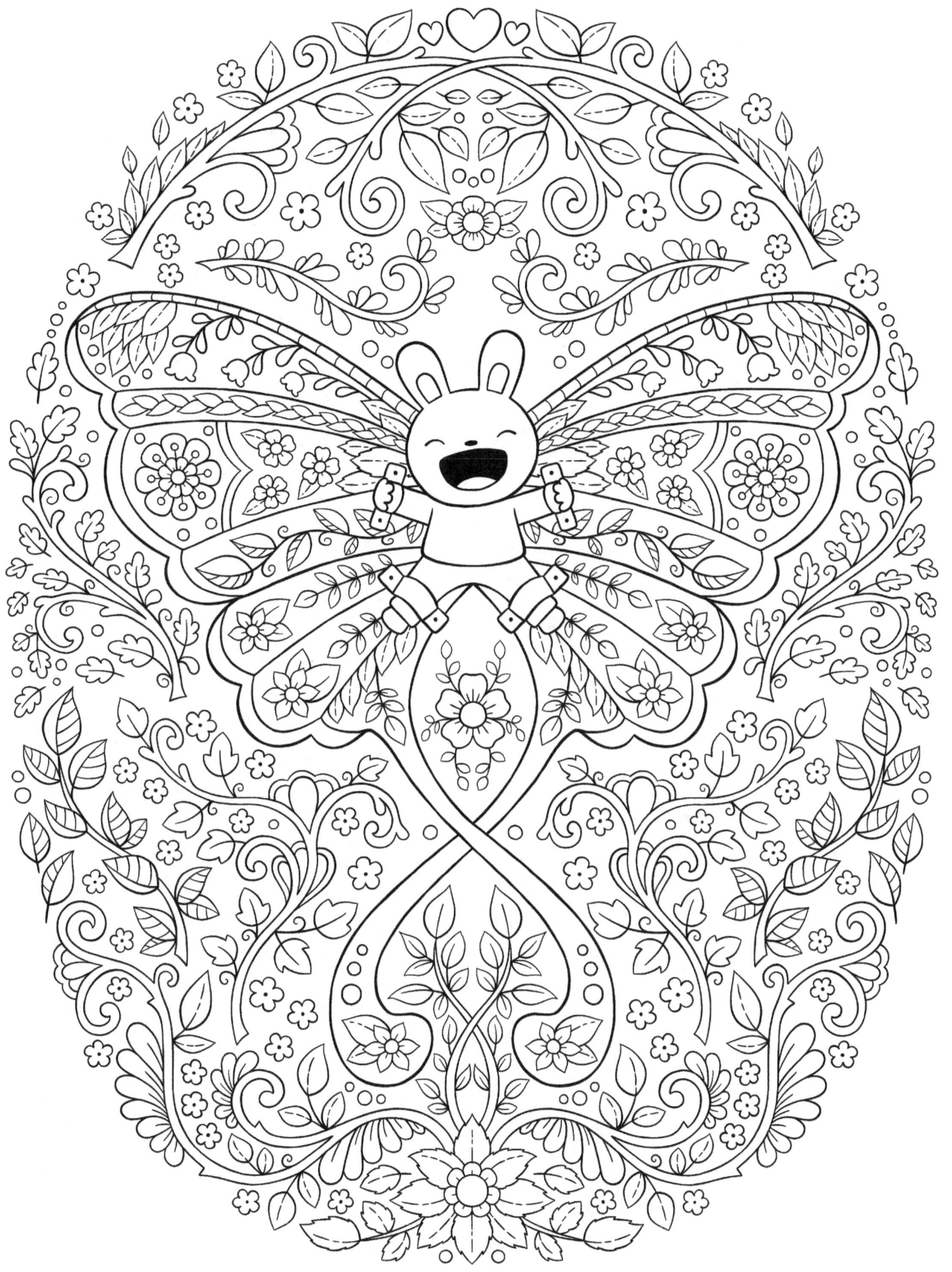

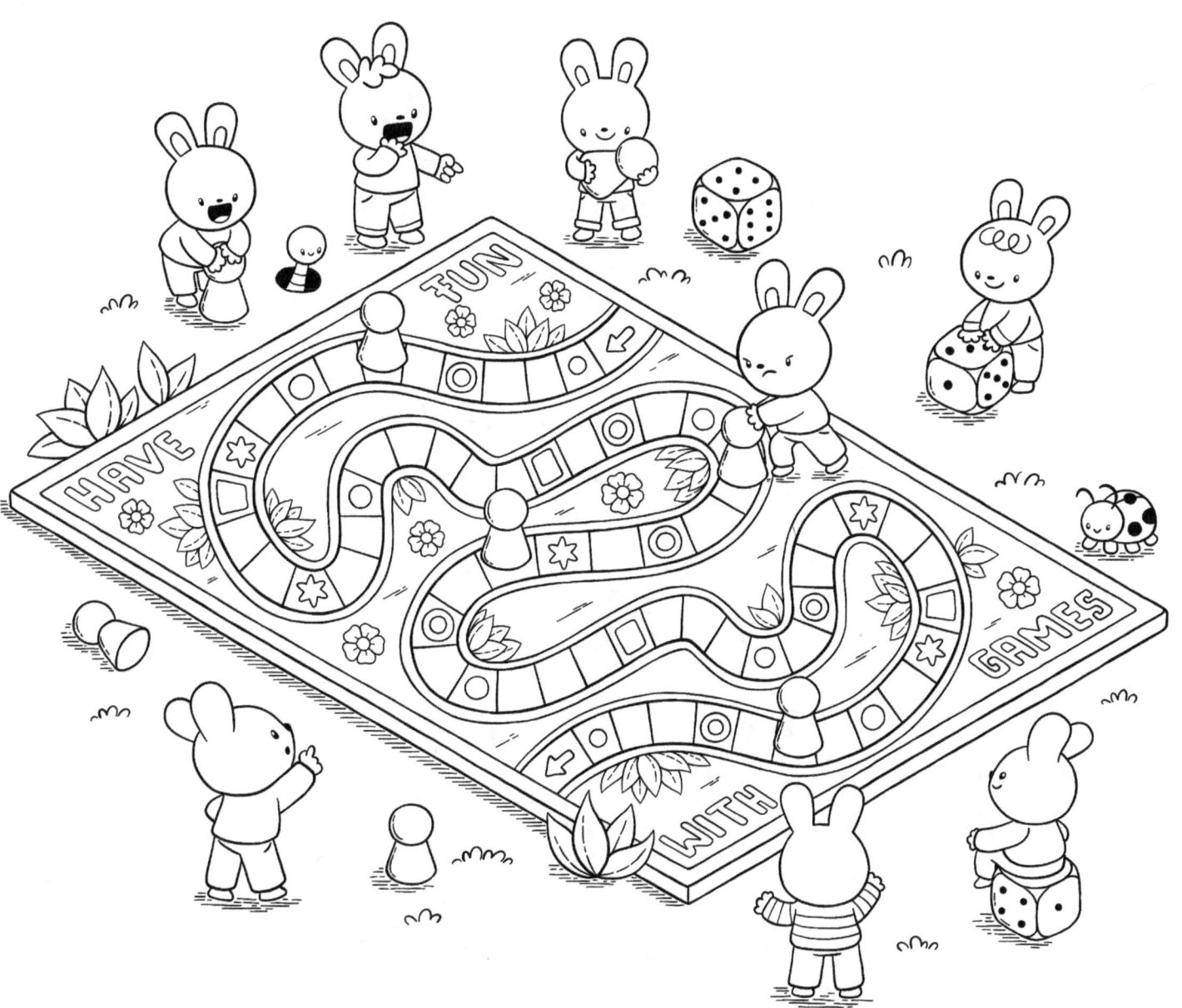

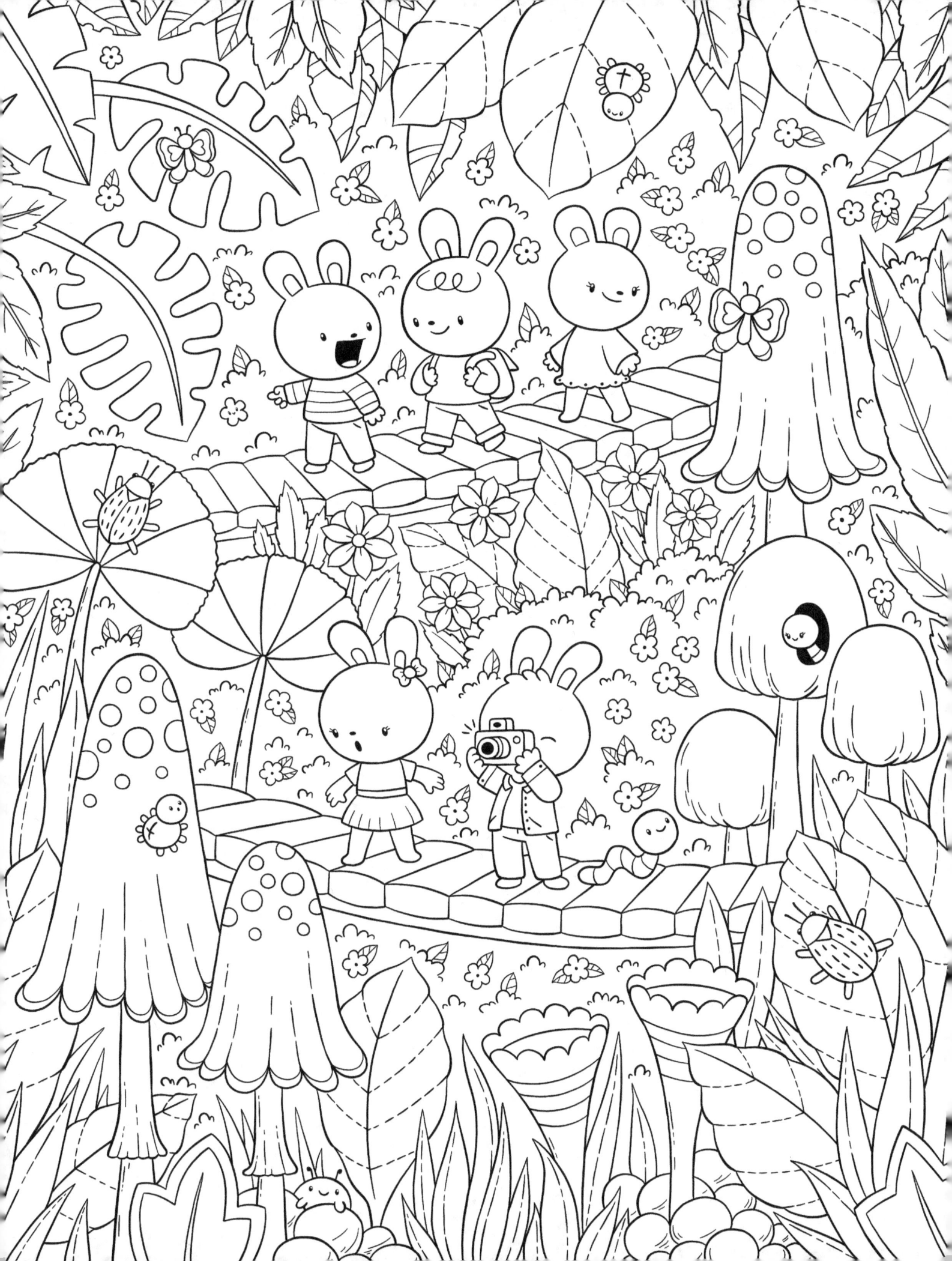

Here begins the second part

The second part of the book contains copies of the illustrations. This gives you the opportunity to color the pictures again through colors or other techniques. However, the outlines are gray, which gives you two more options:

The lines are so light that they are easy to paint over. This allows you to create a picture without any dark edges at the end.

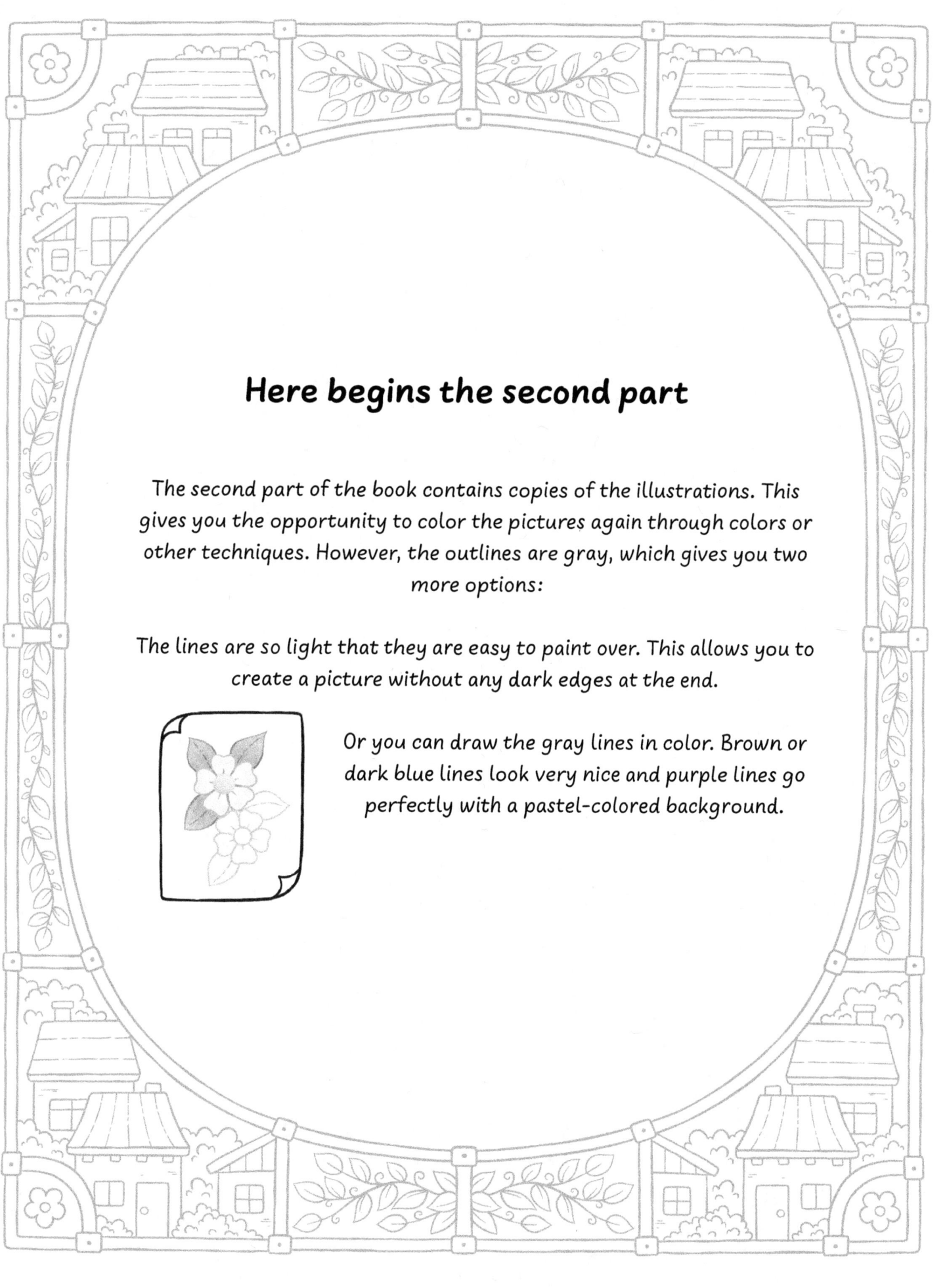

Or you can draw the gray lines in color. Brown or dark blue lines look very nice and purple lines go perfectly with a pastel-colored background.

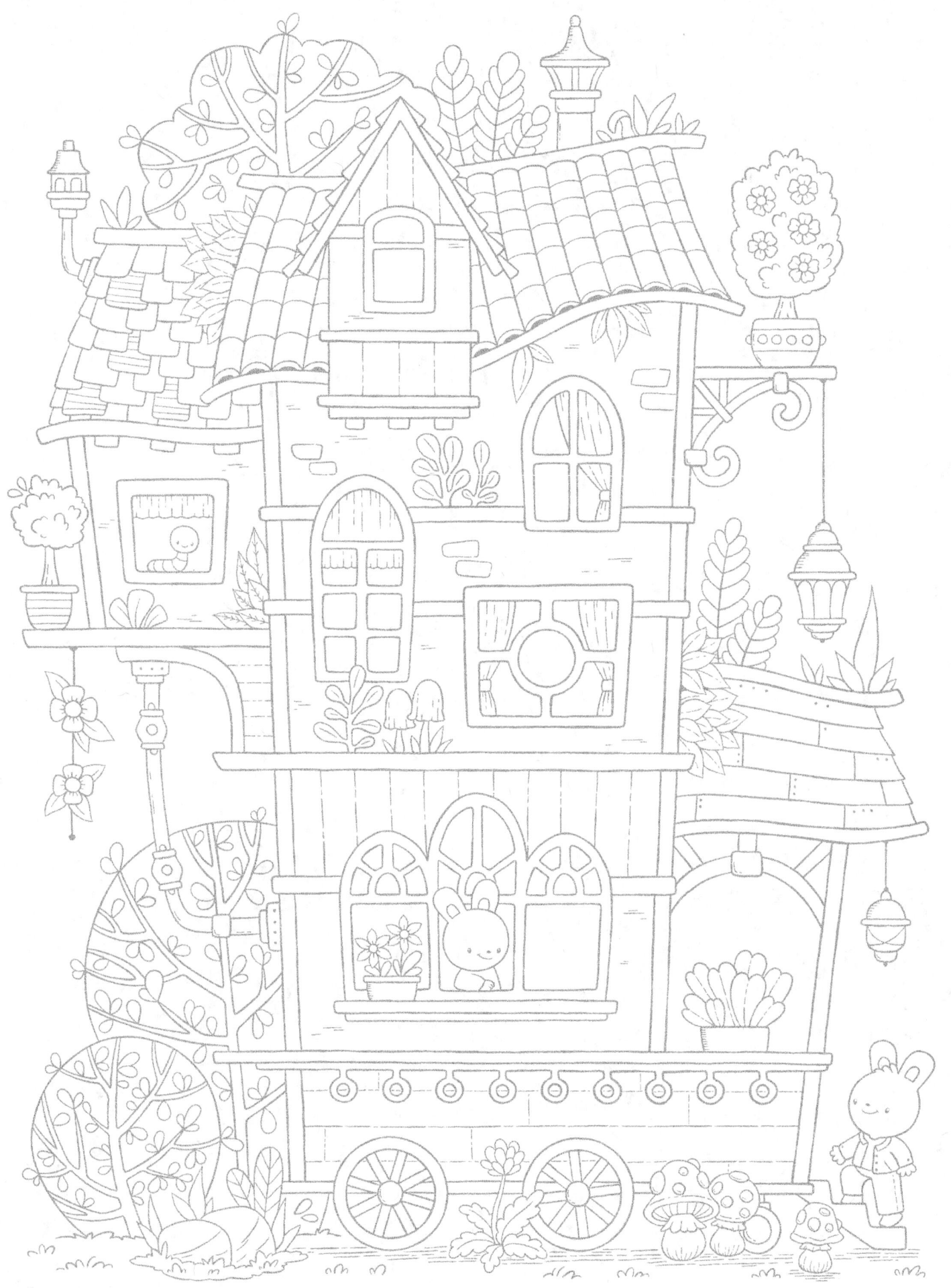

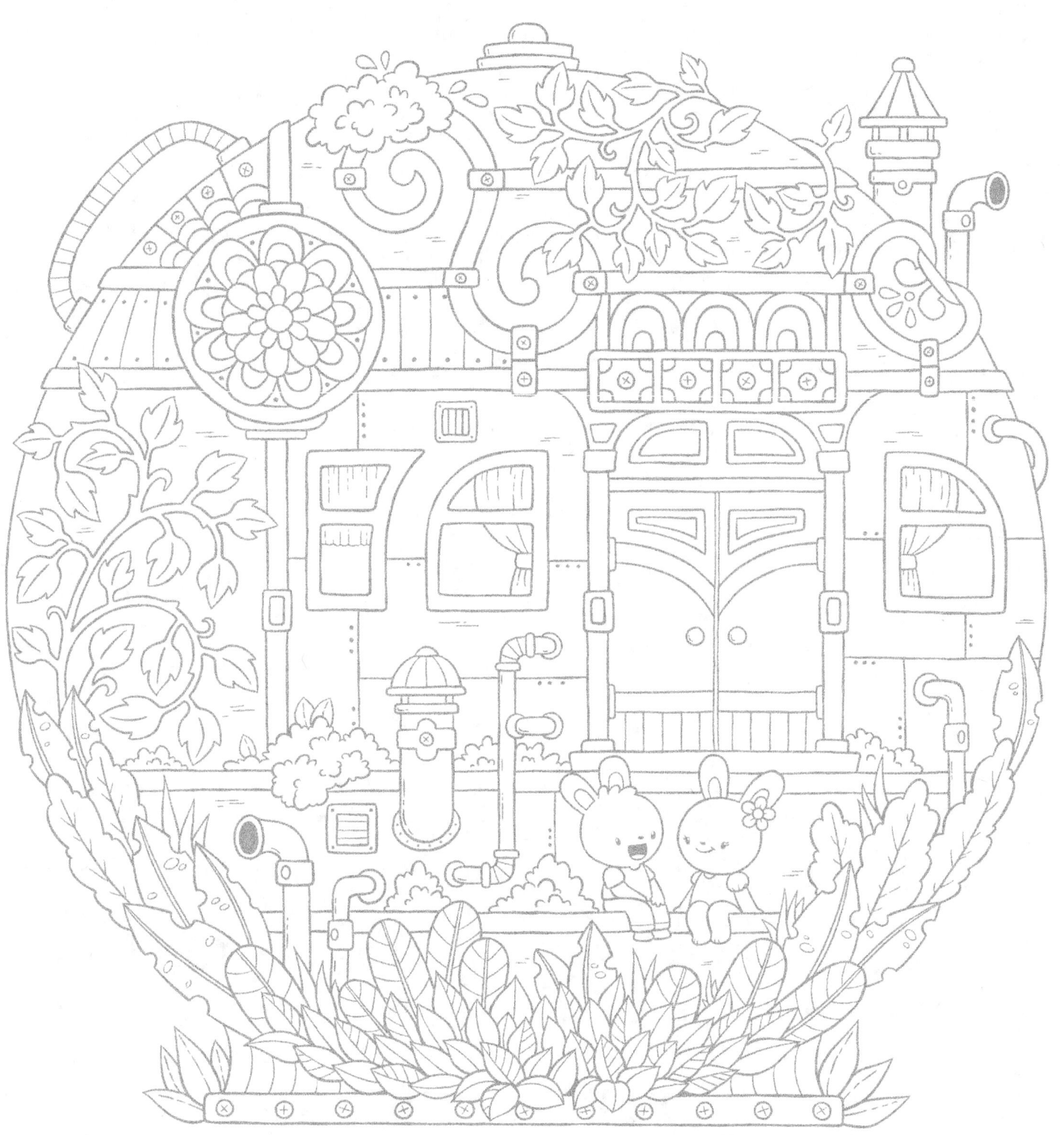

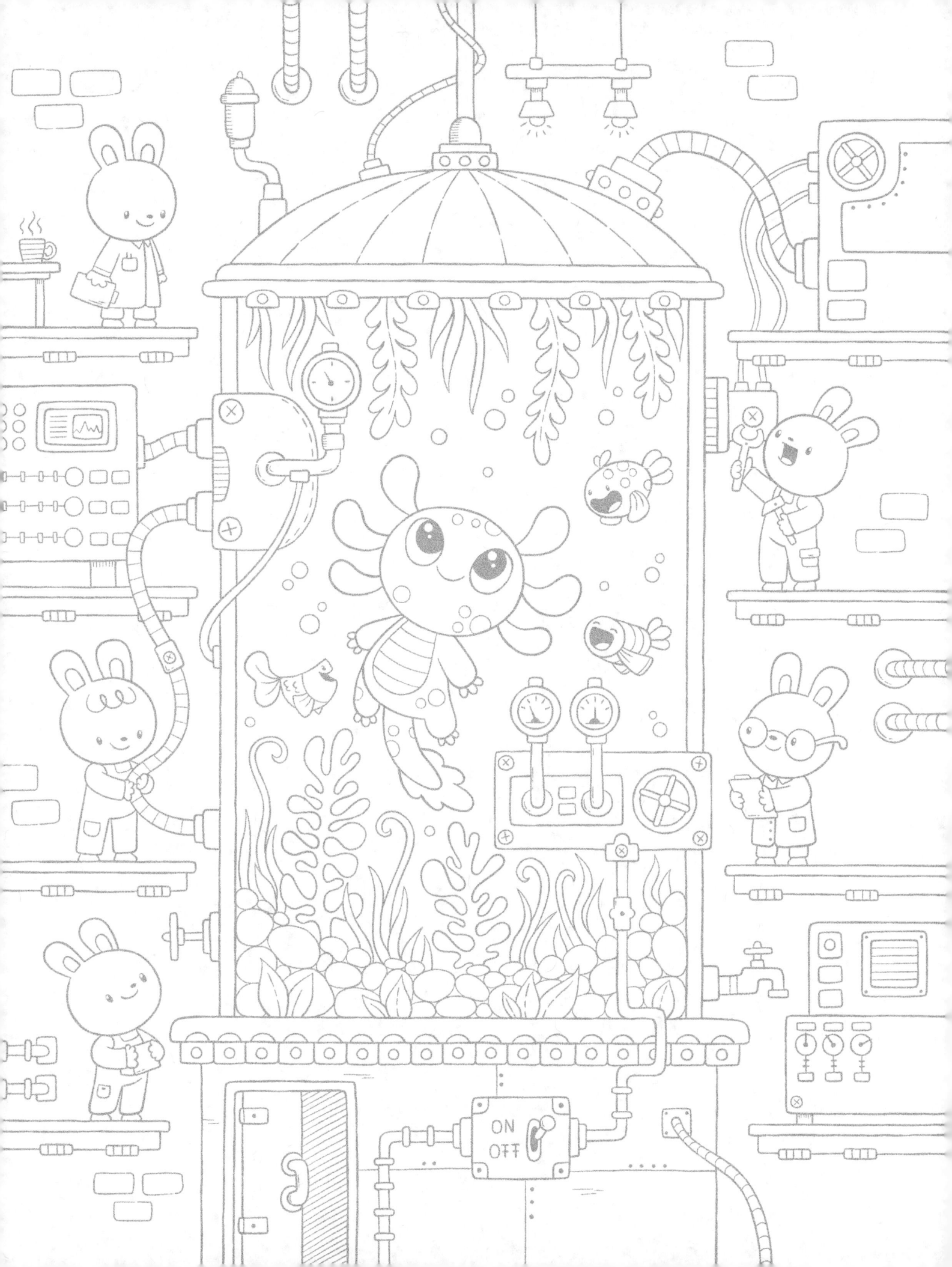

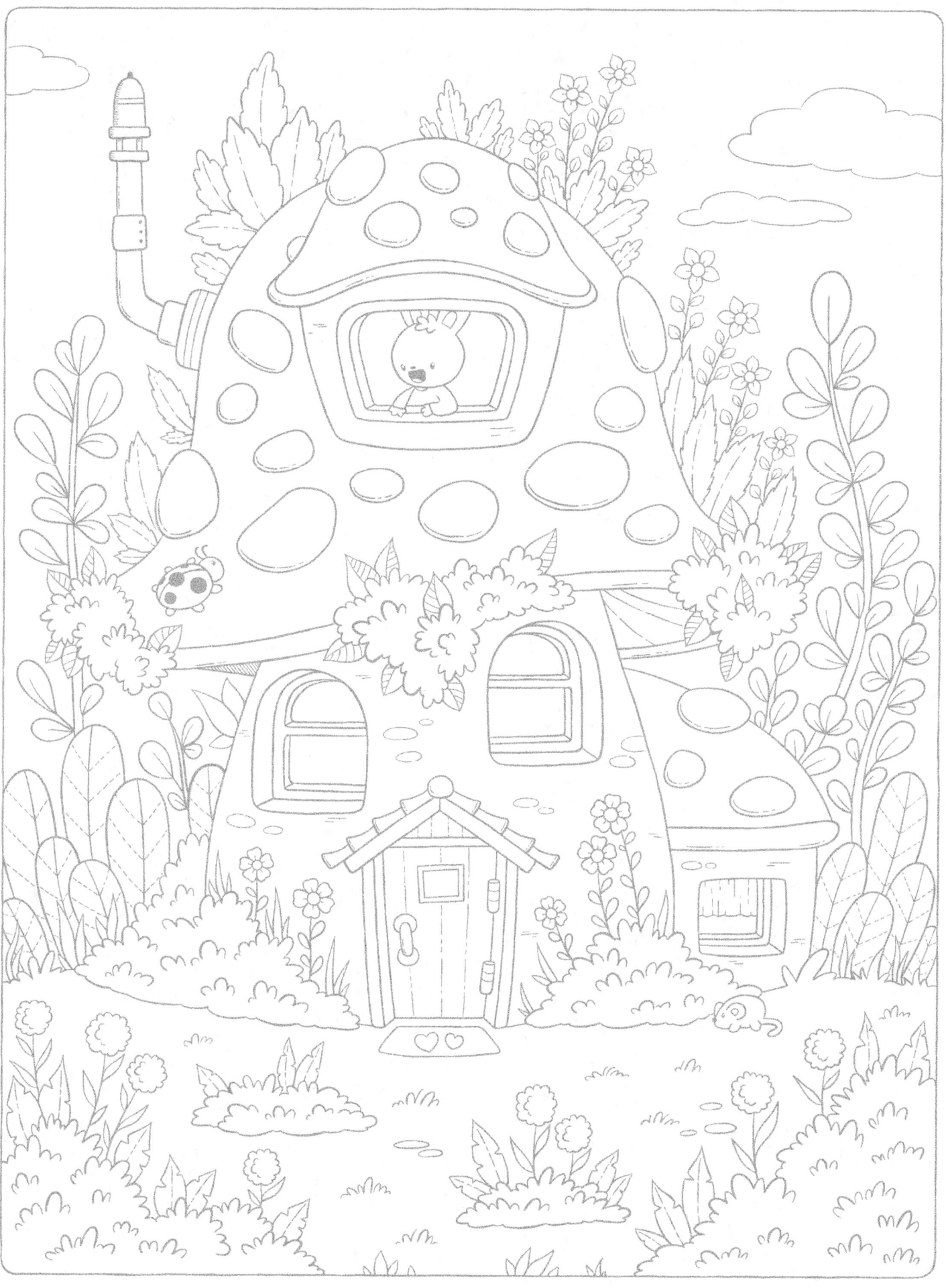

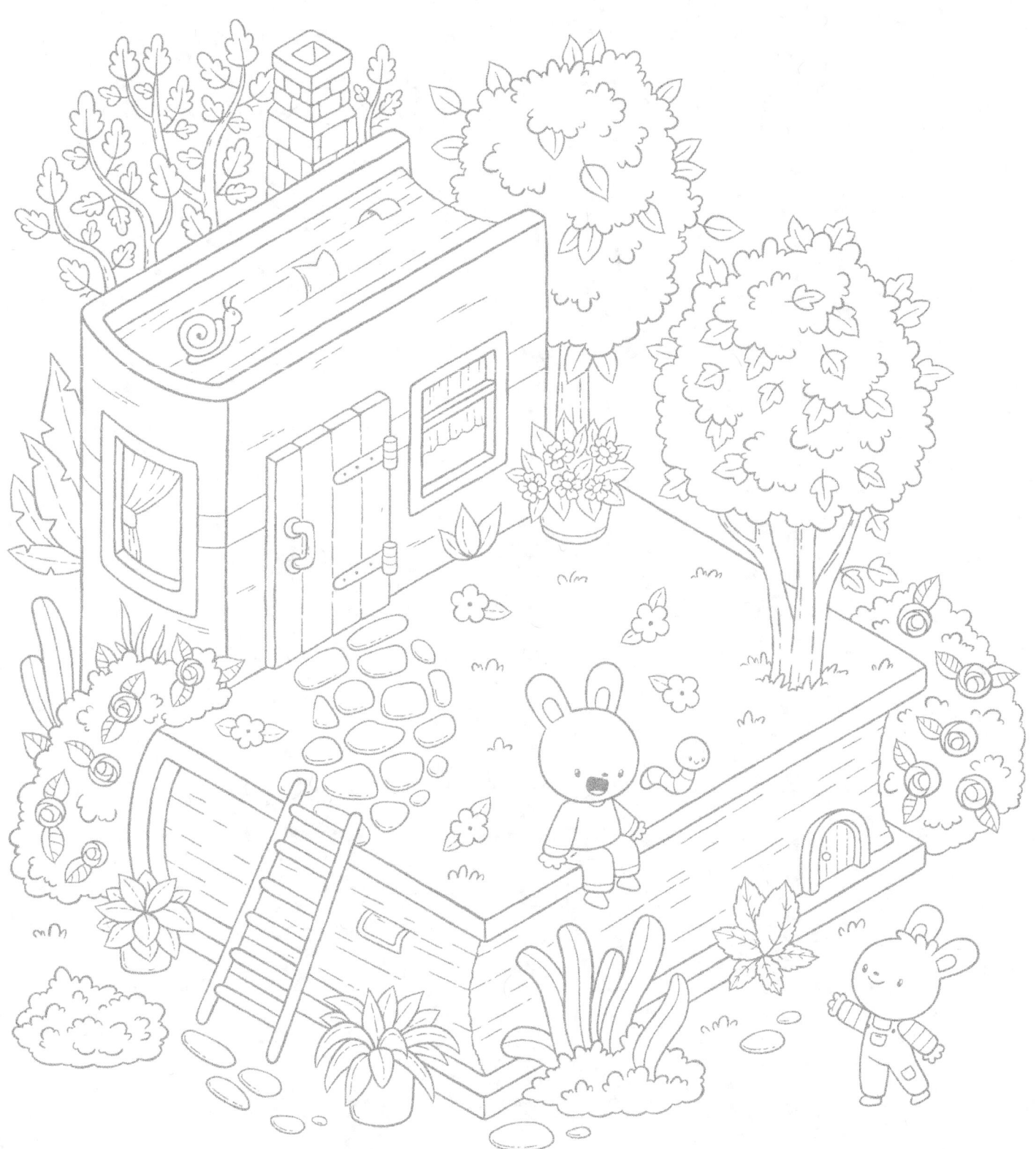

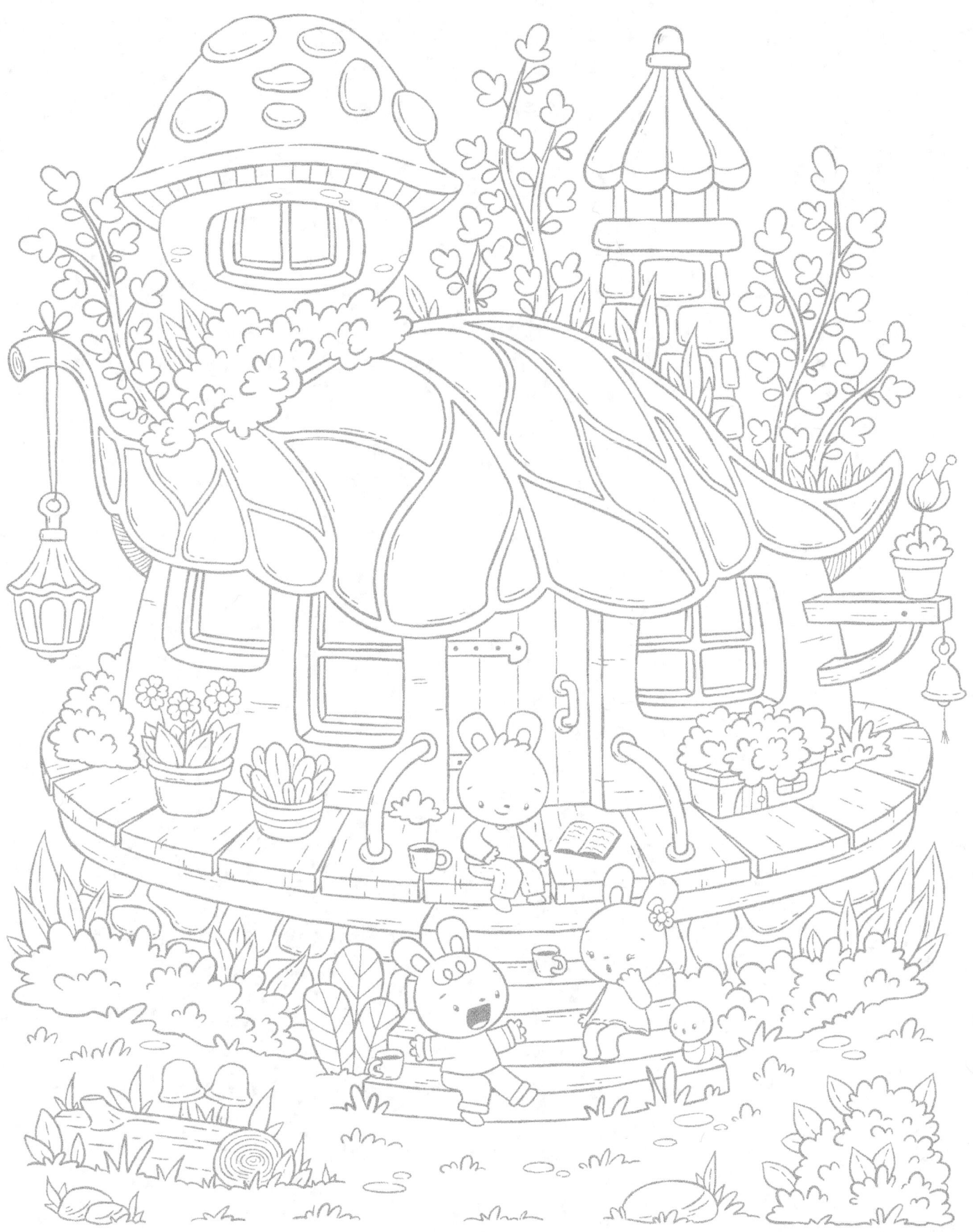

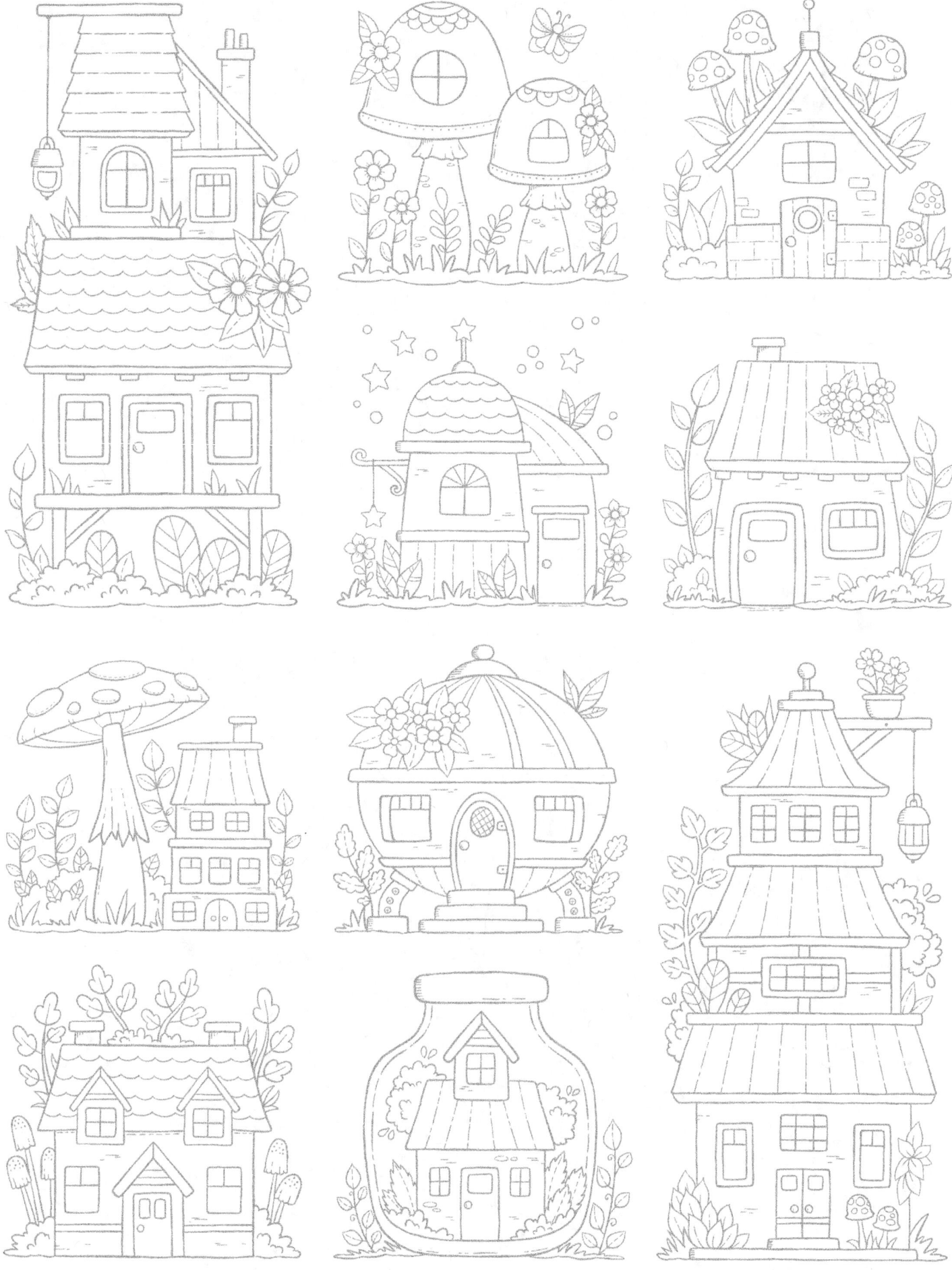

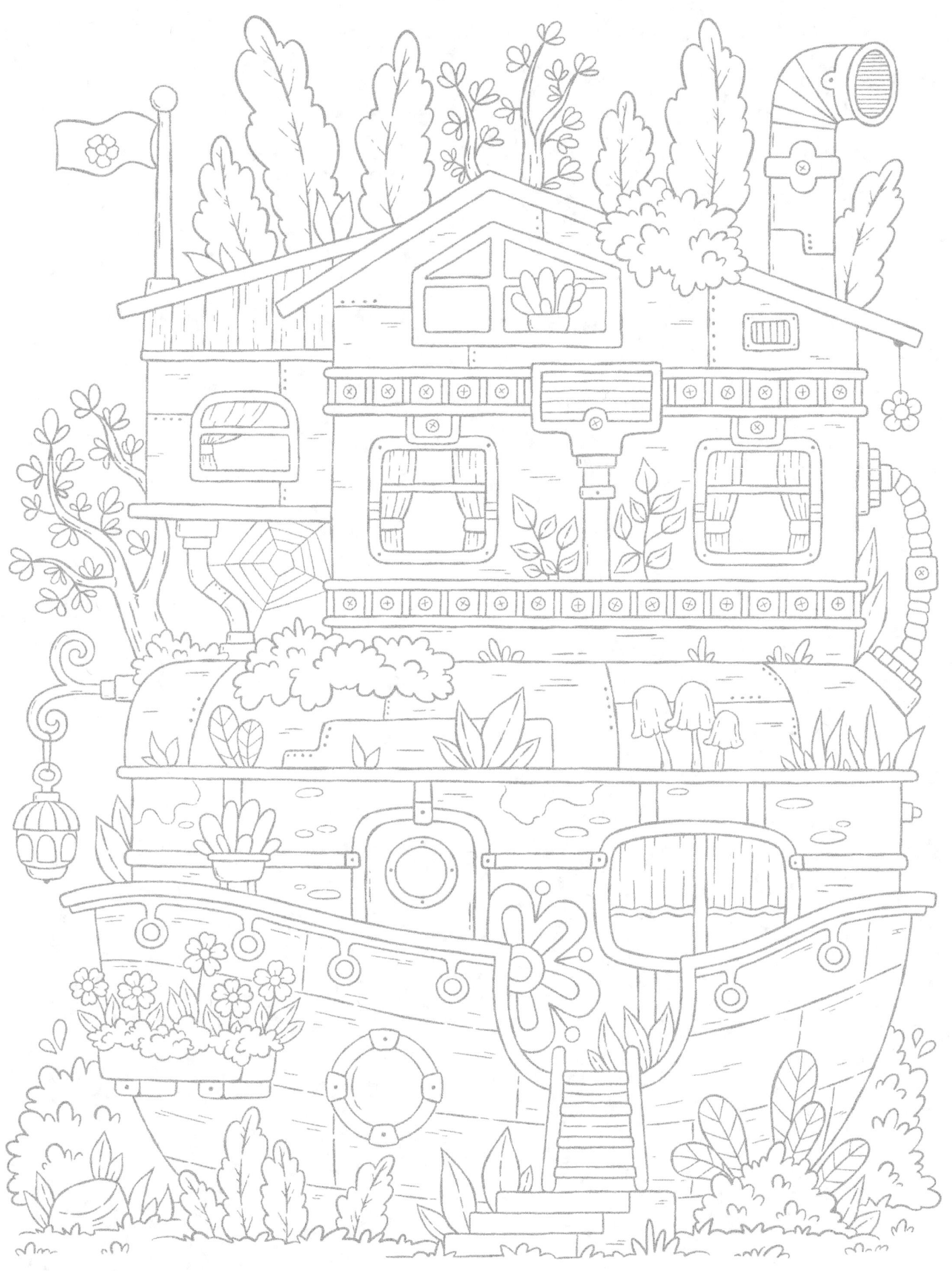

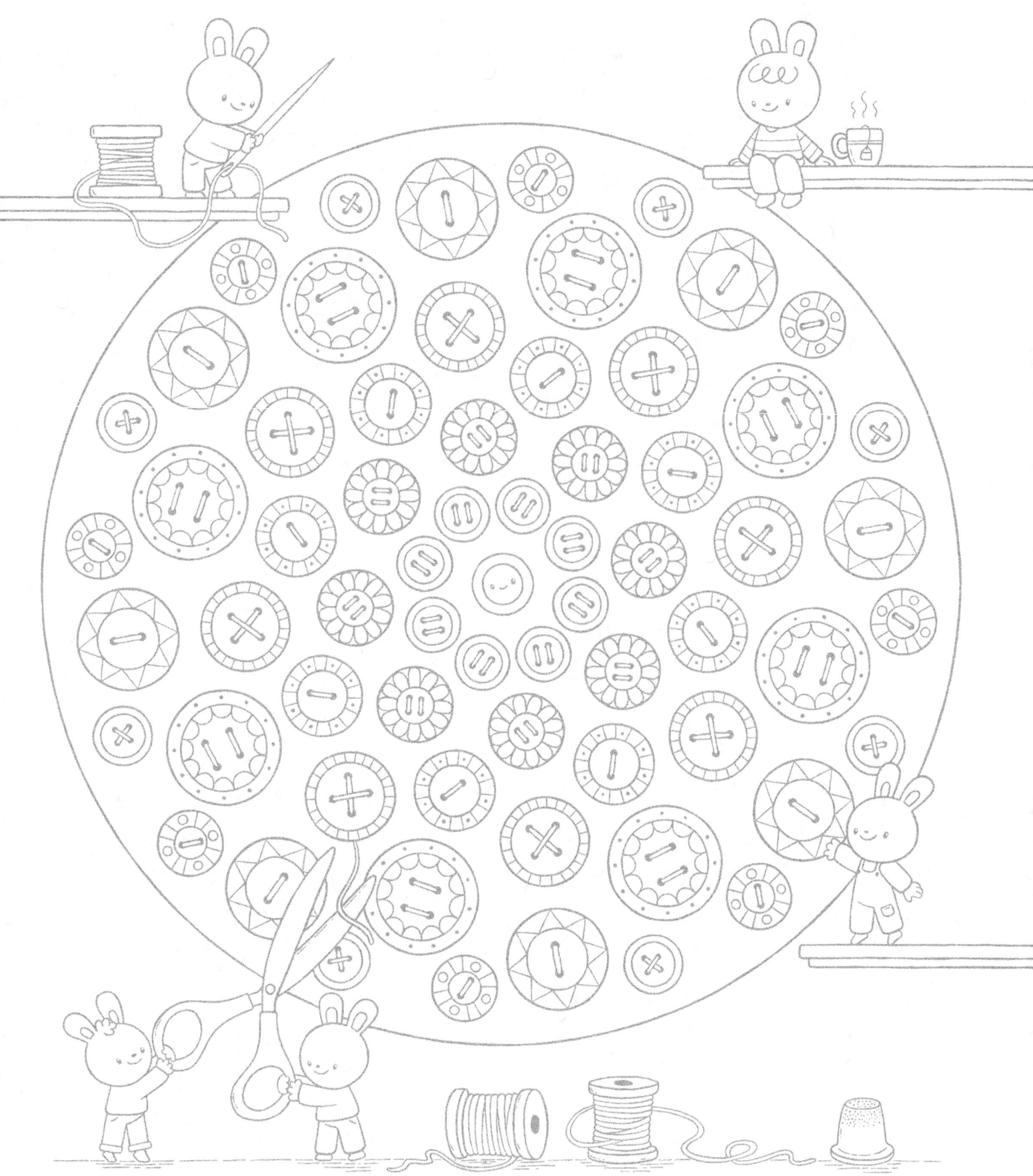

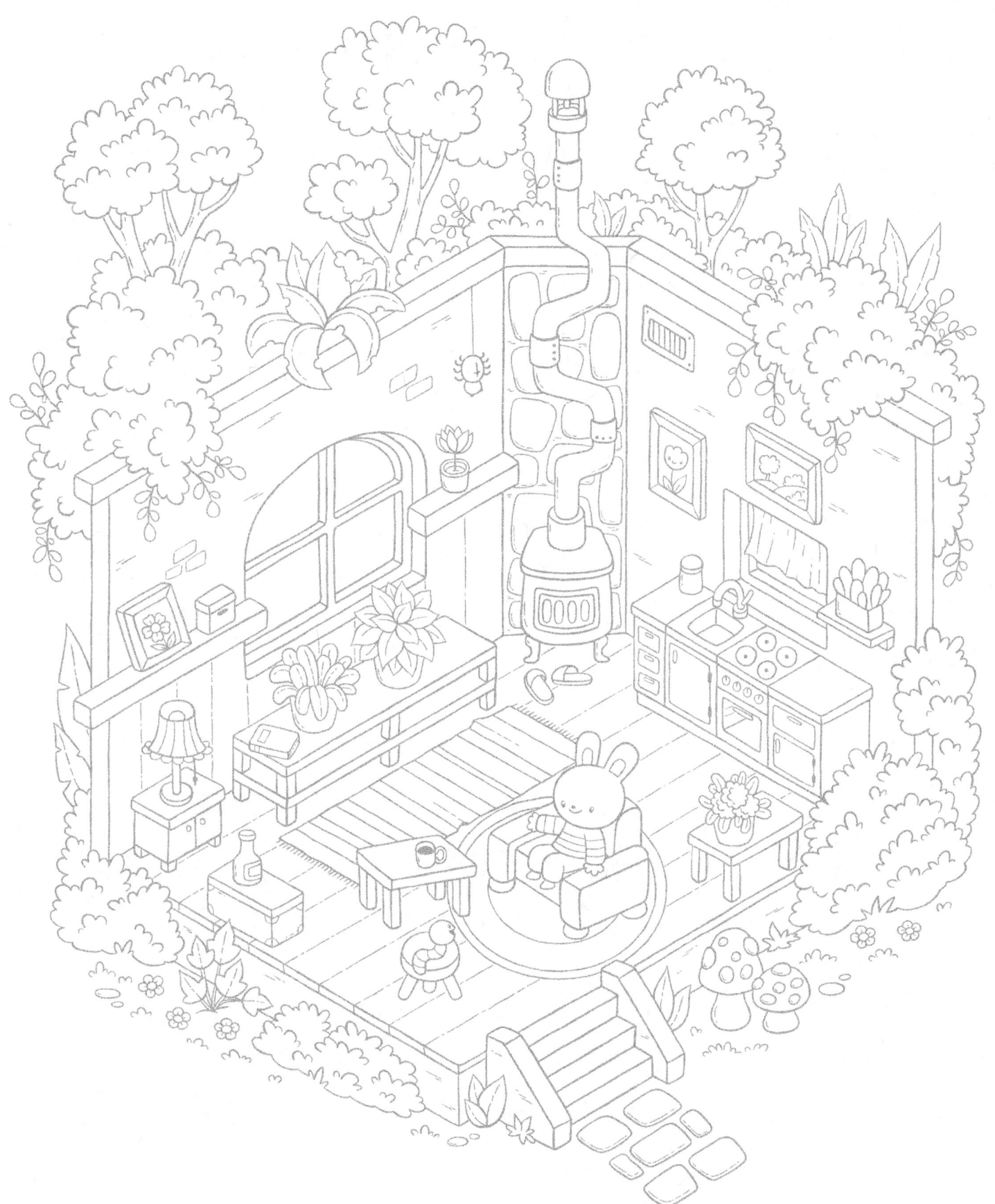

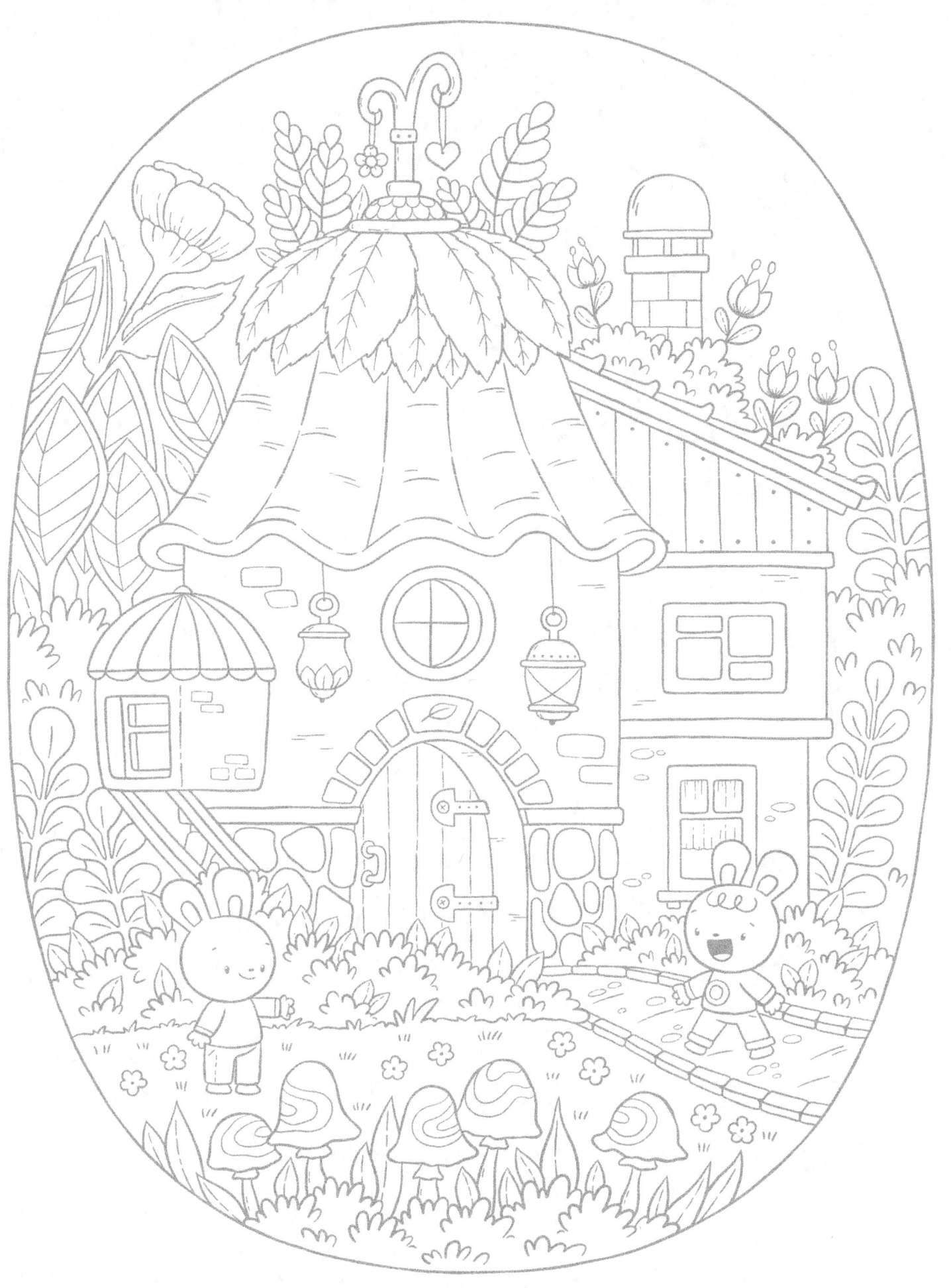

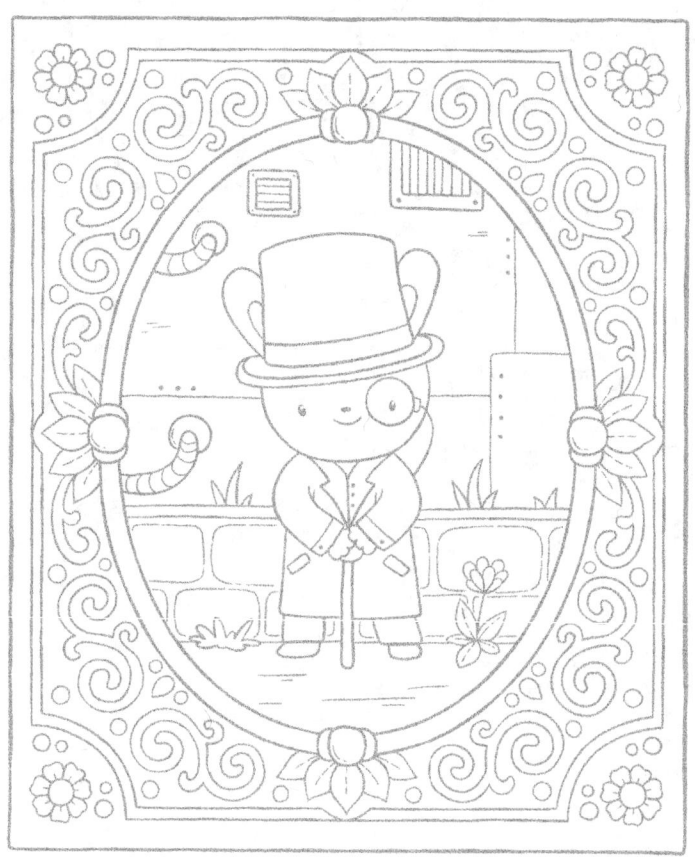
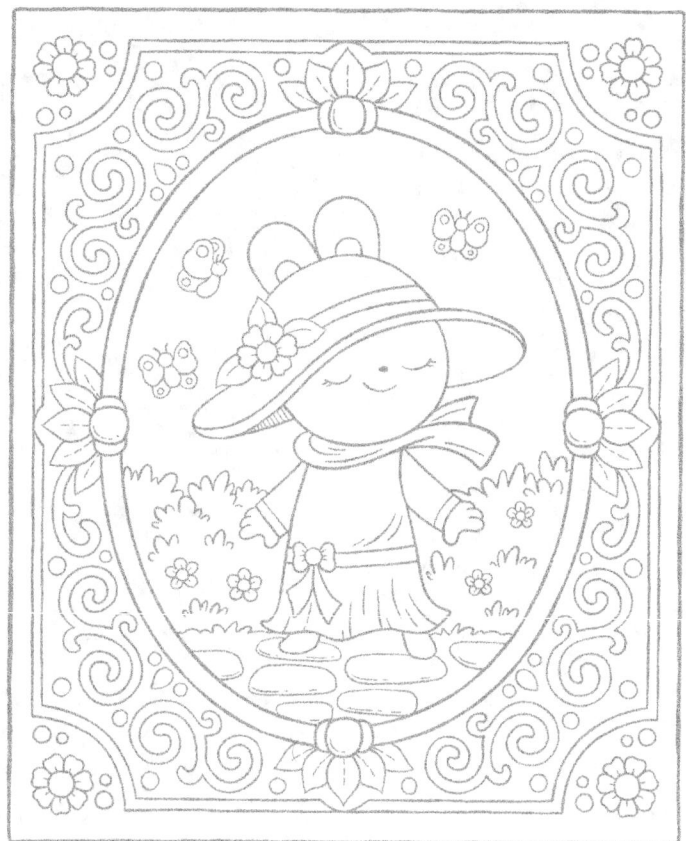
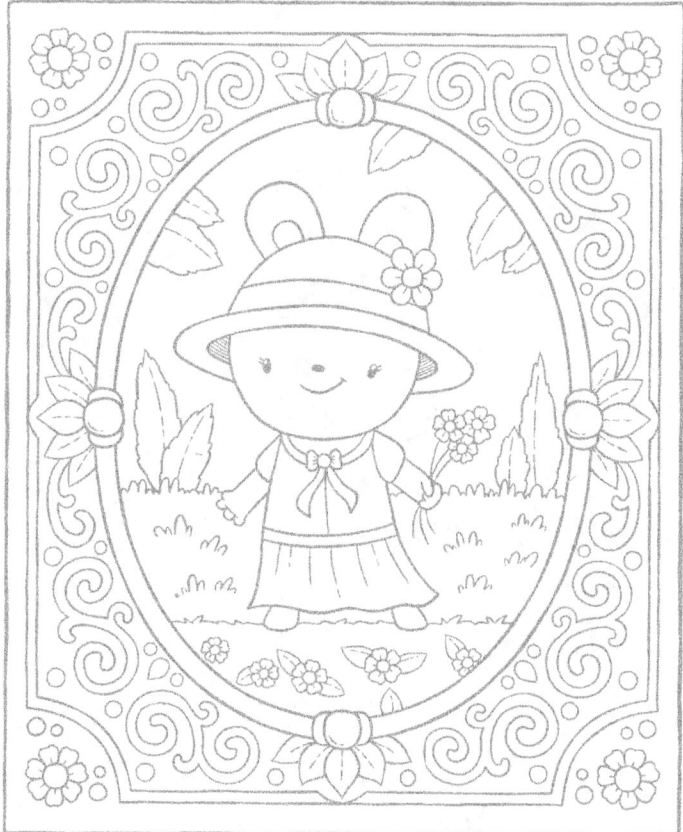
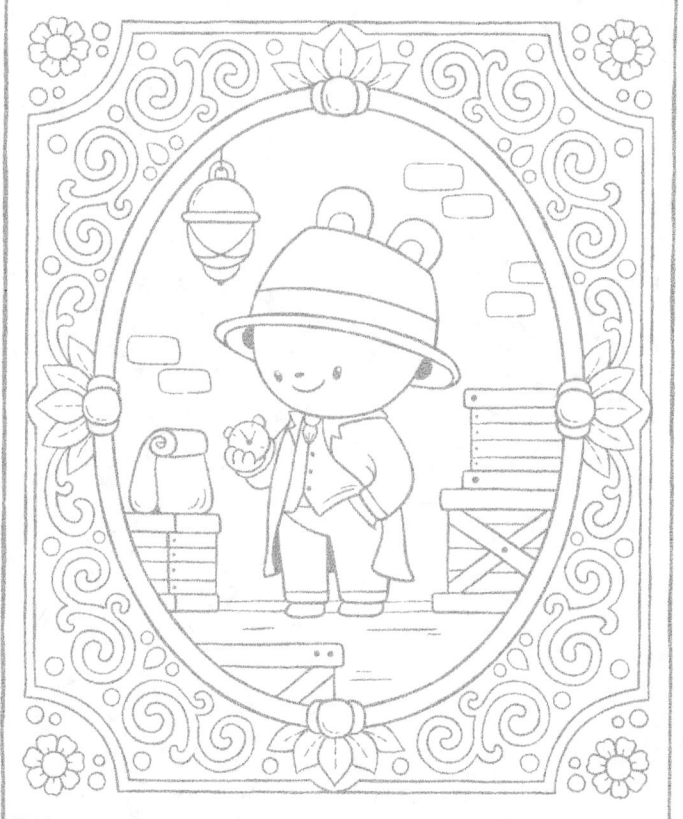

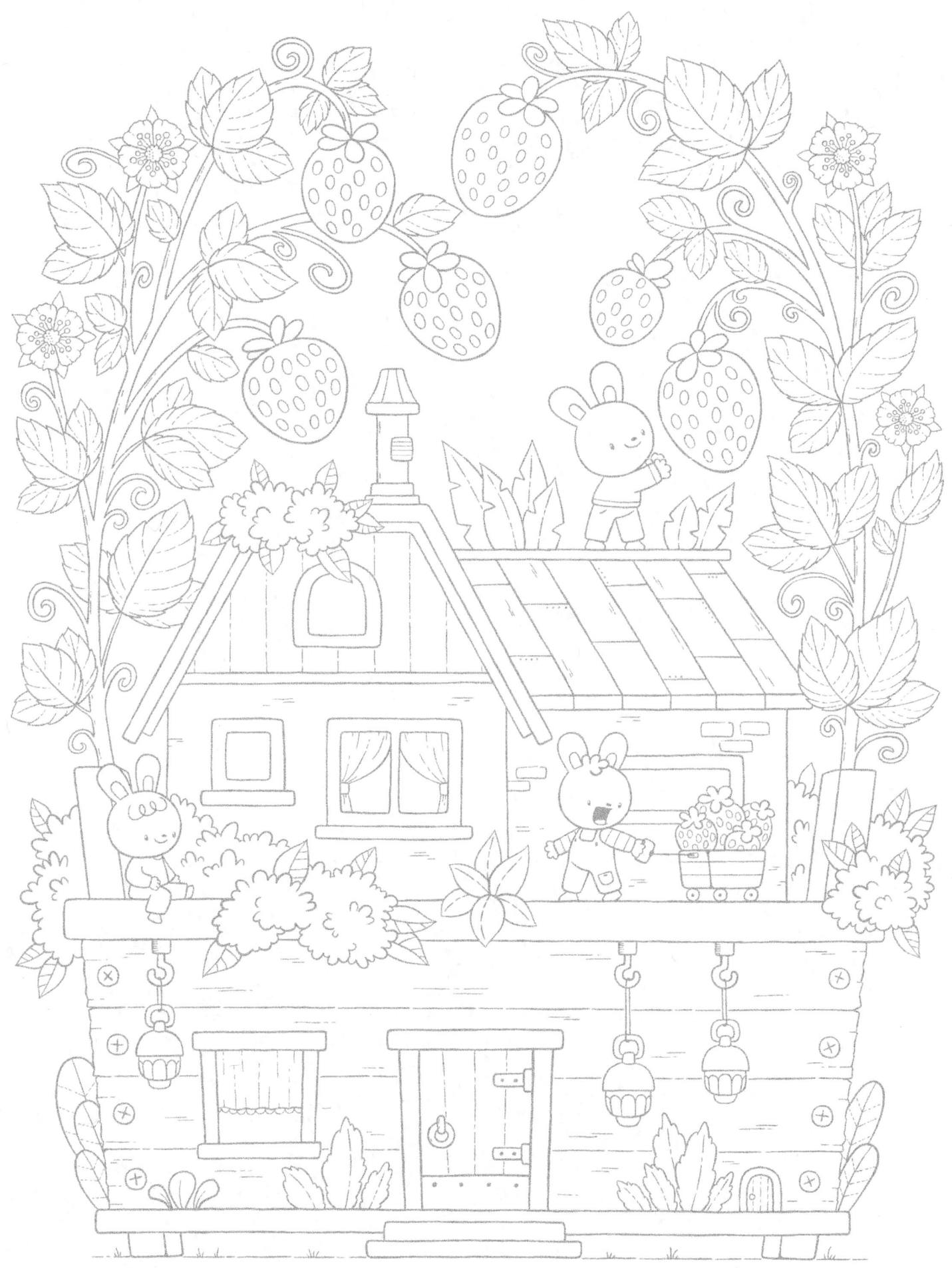

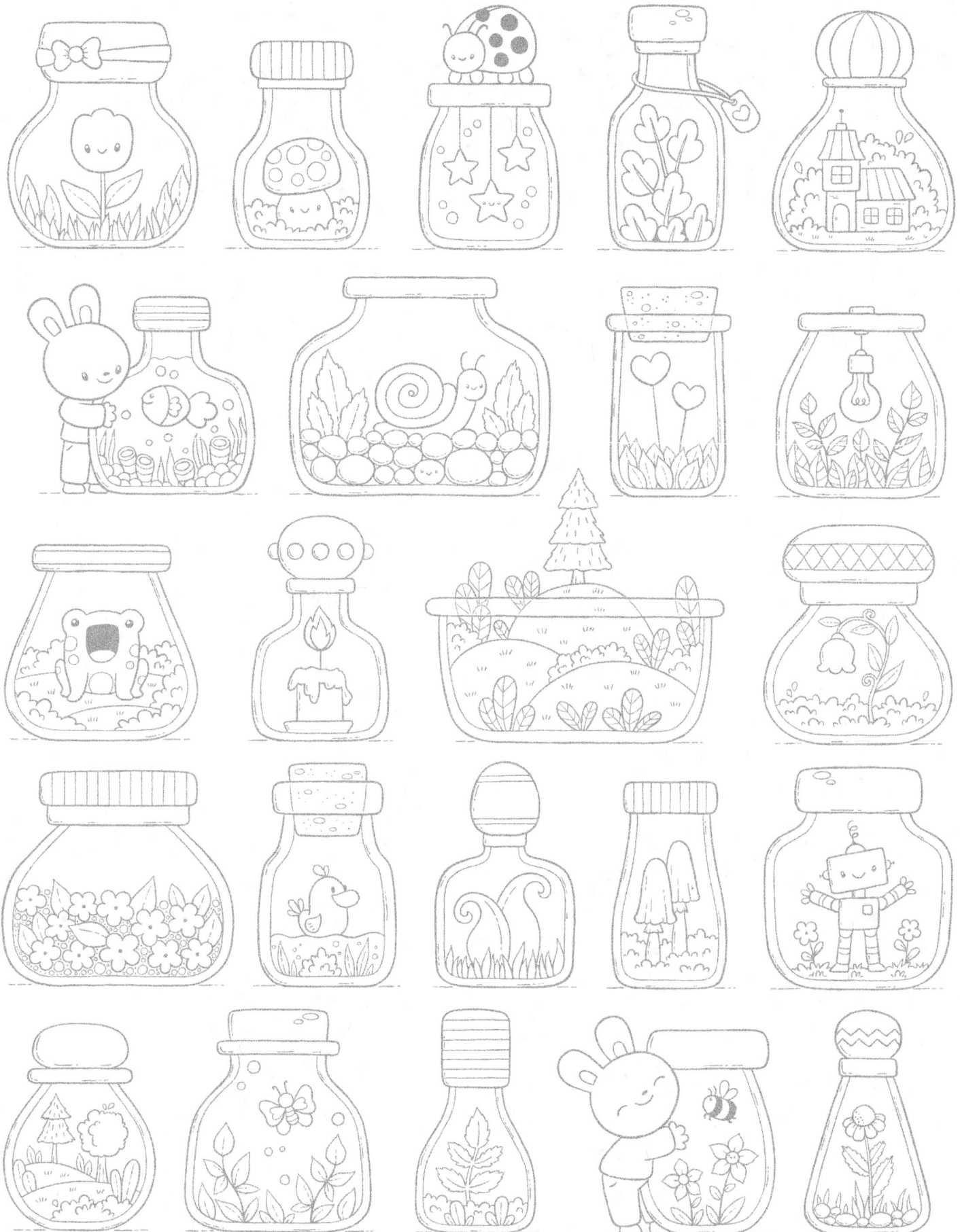

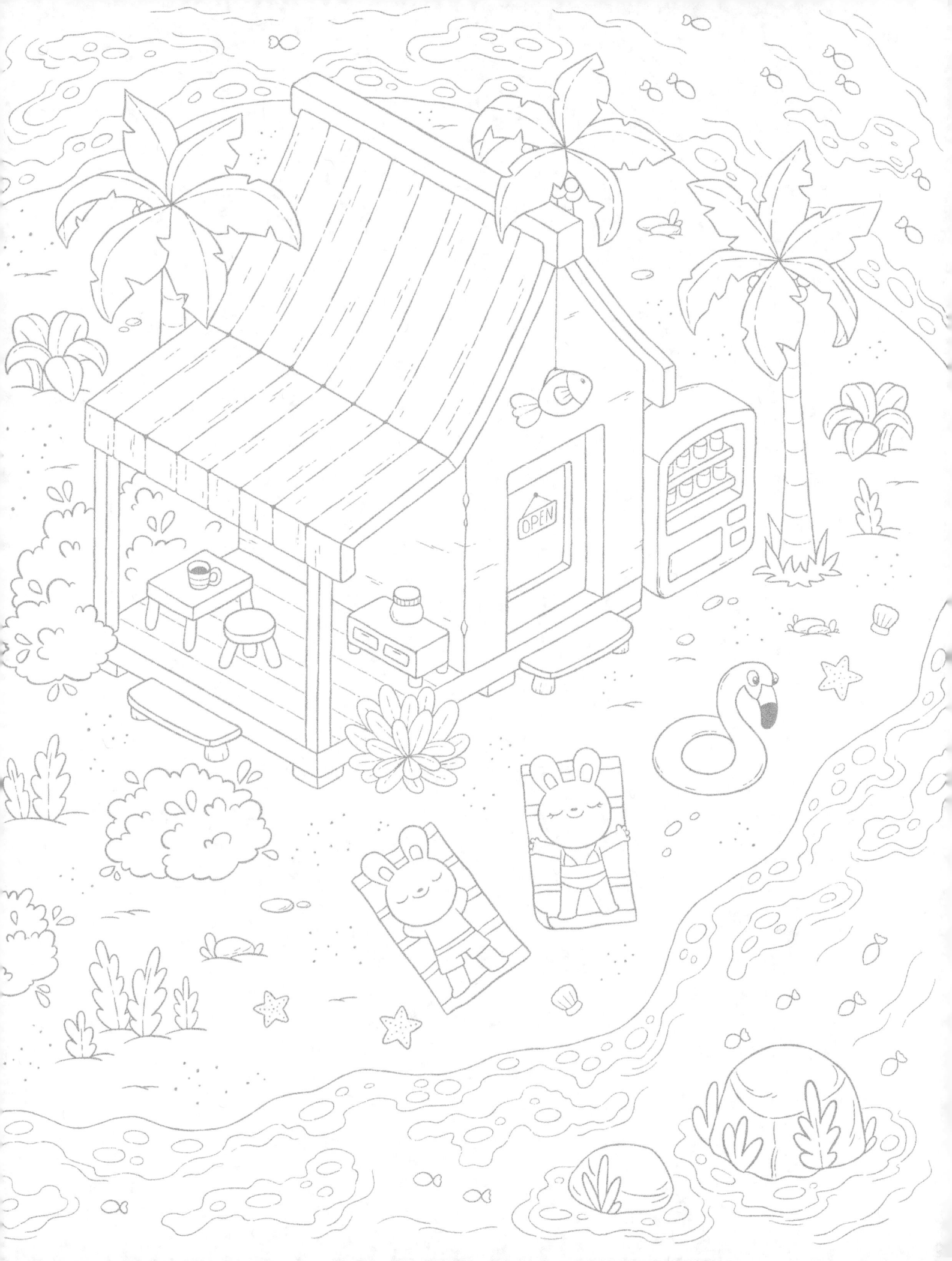

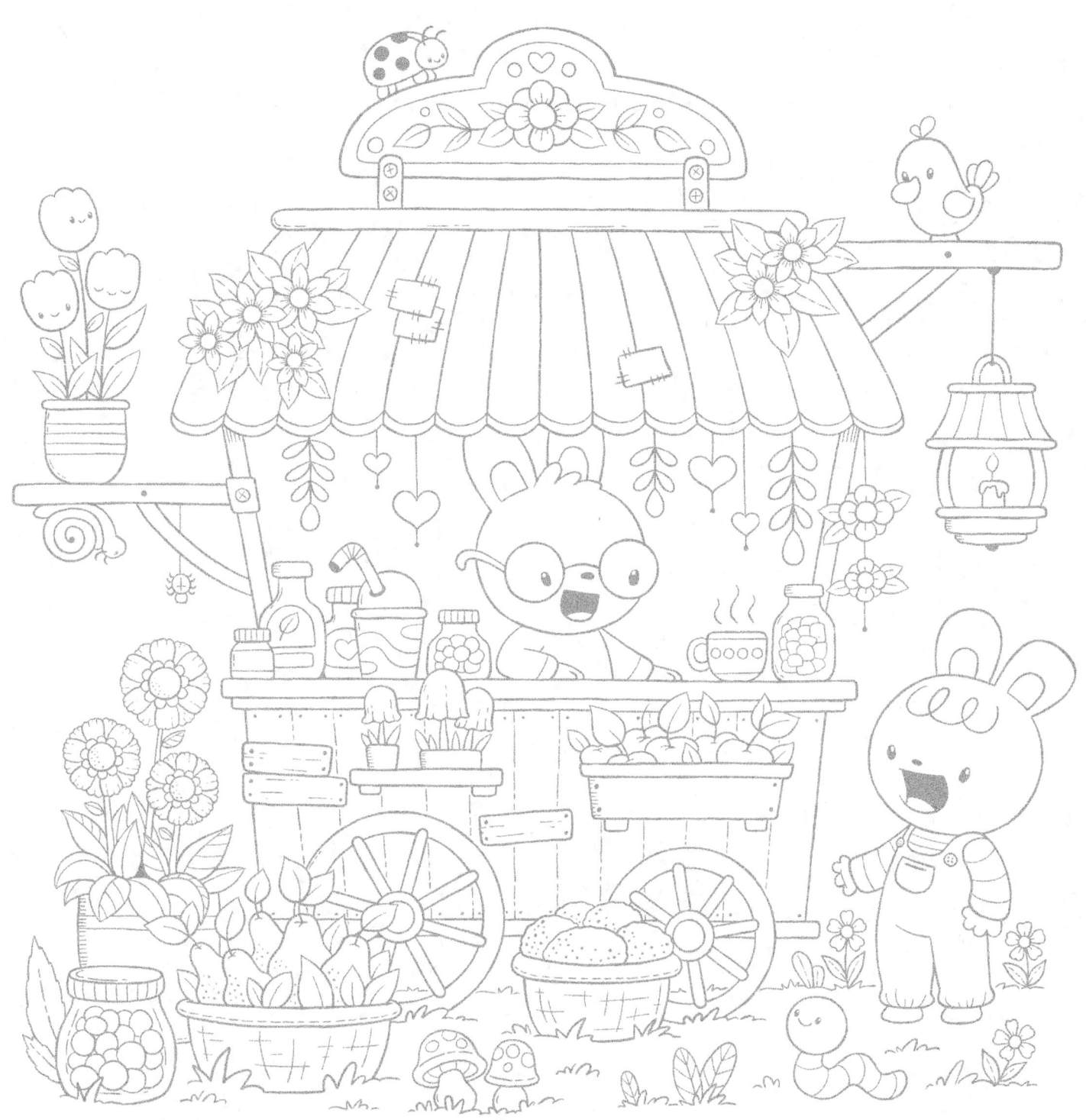

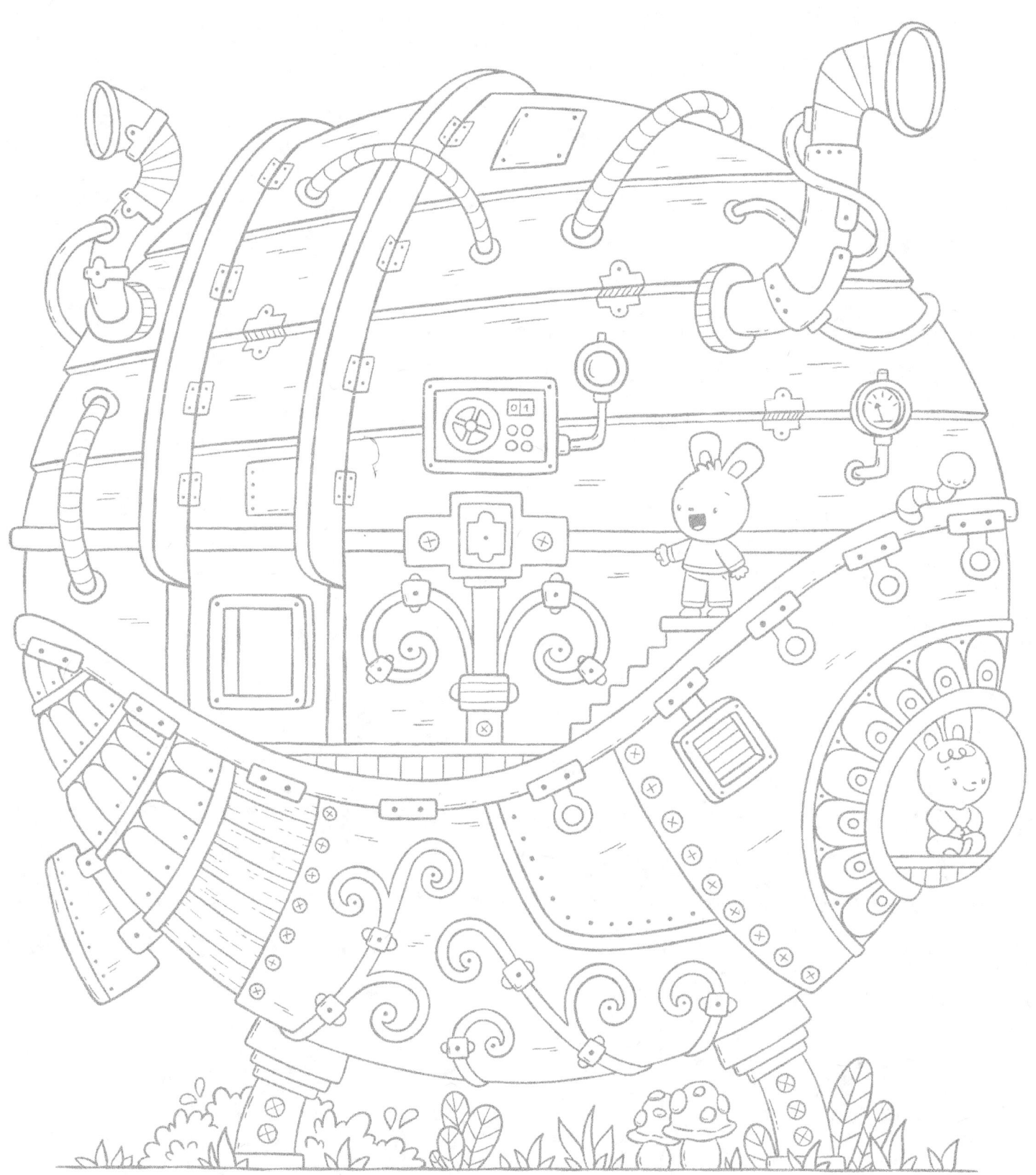

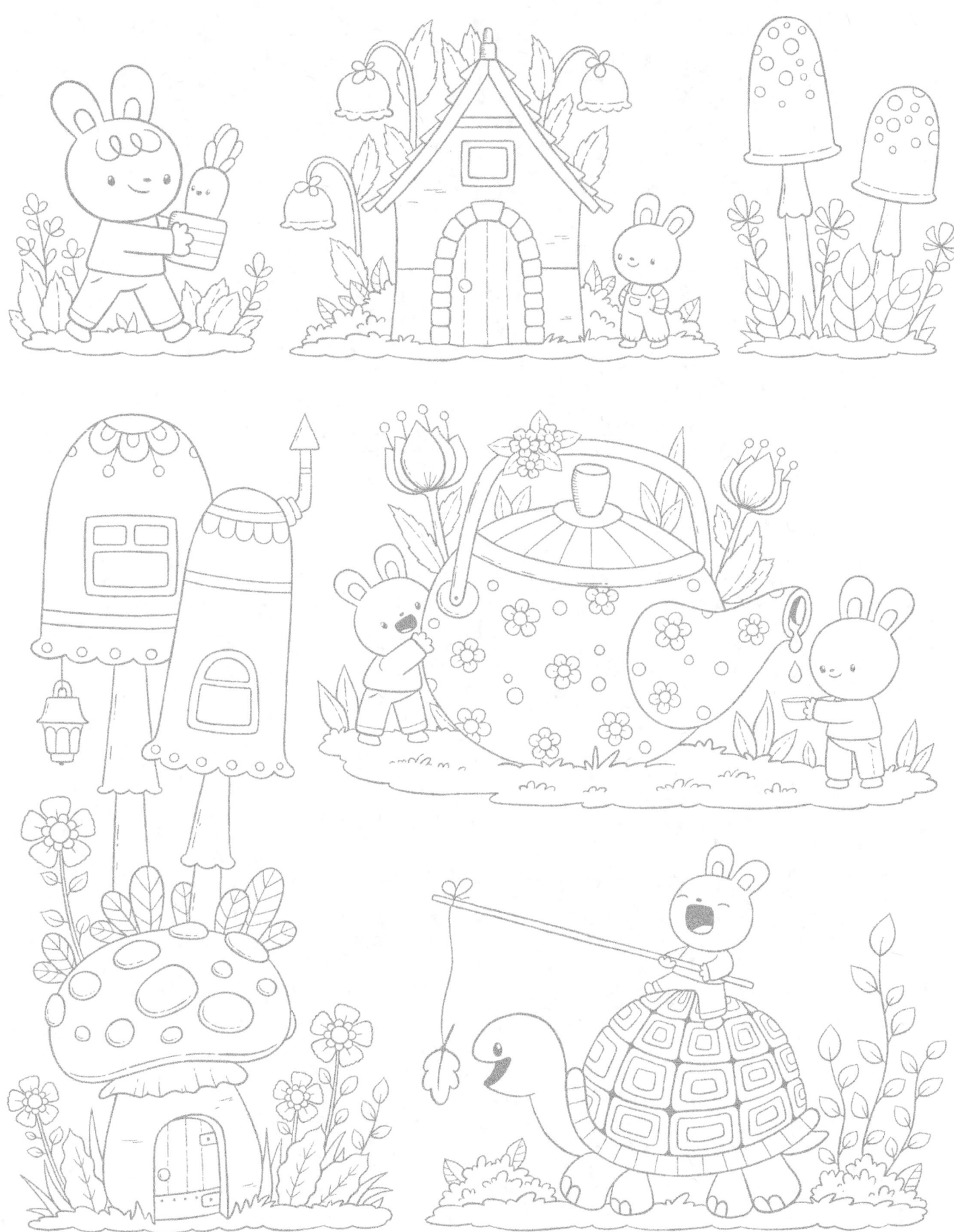

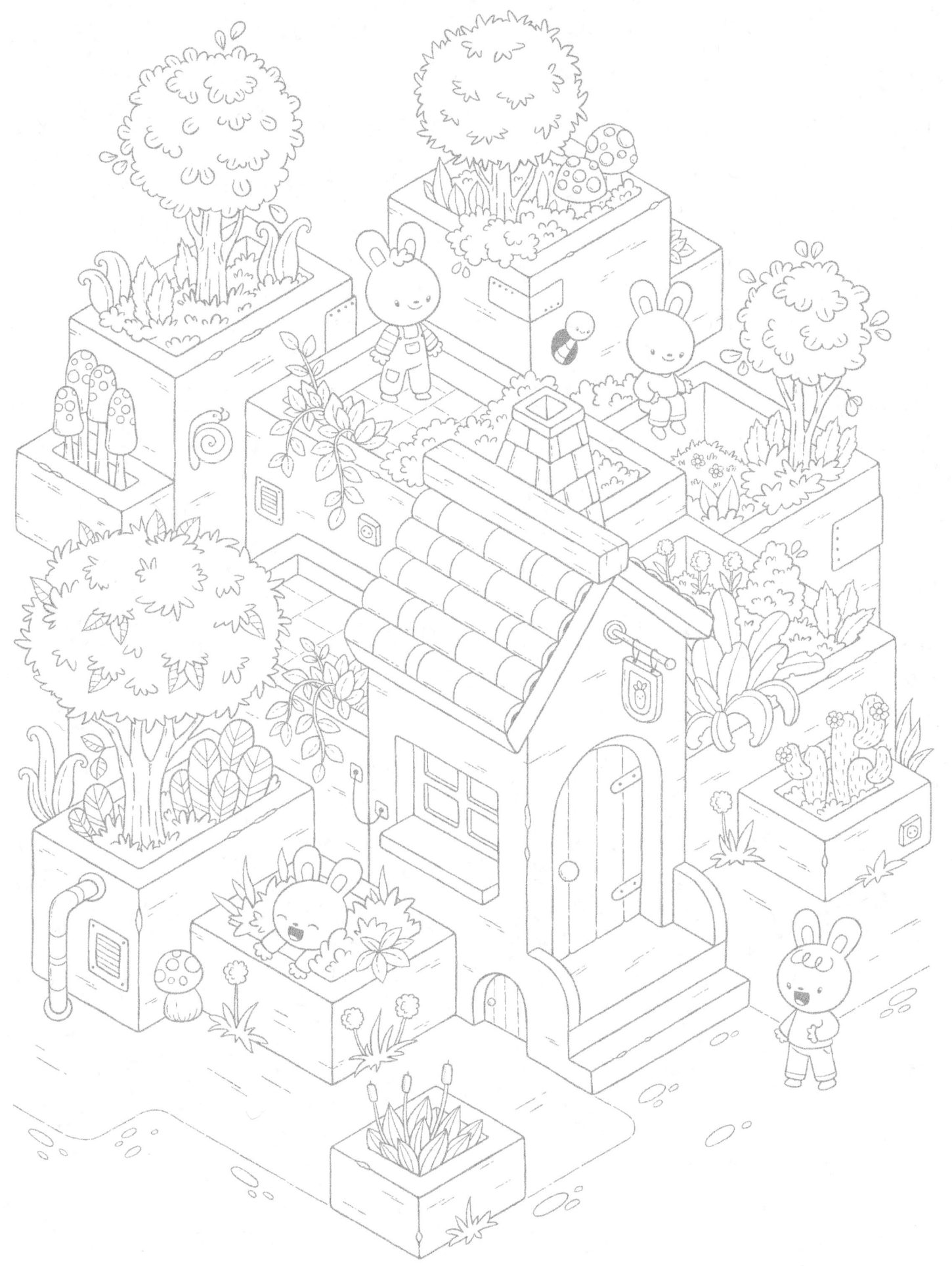

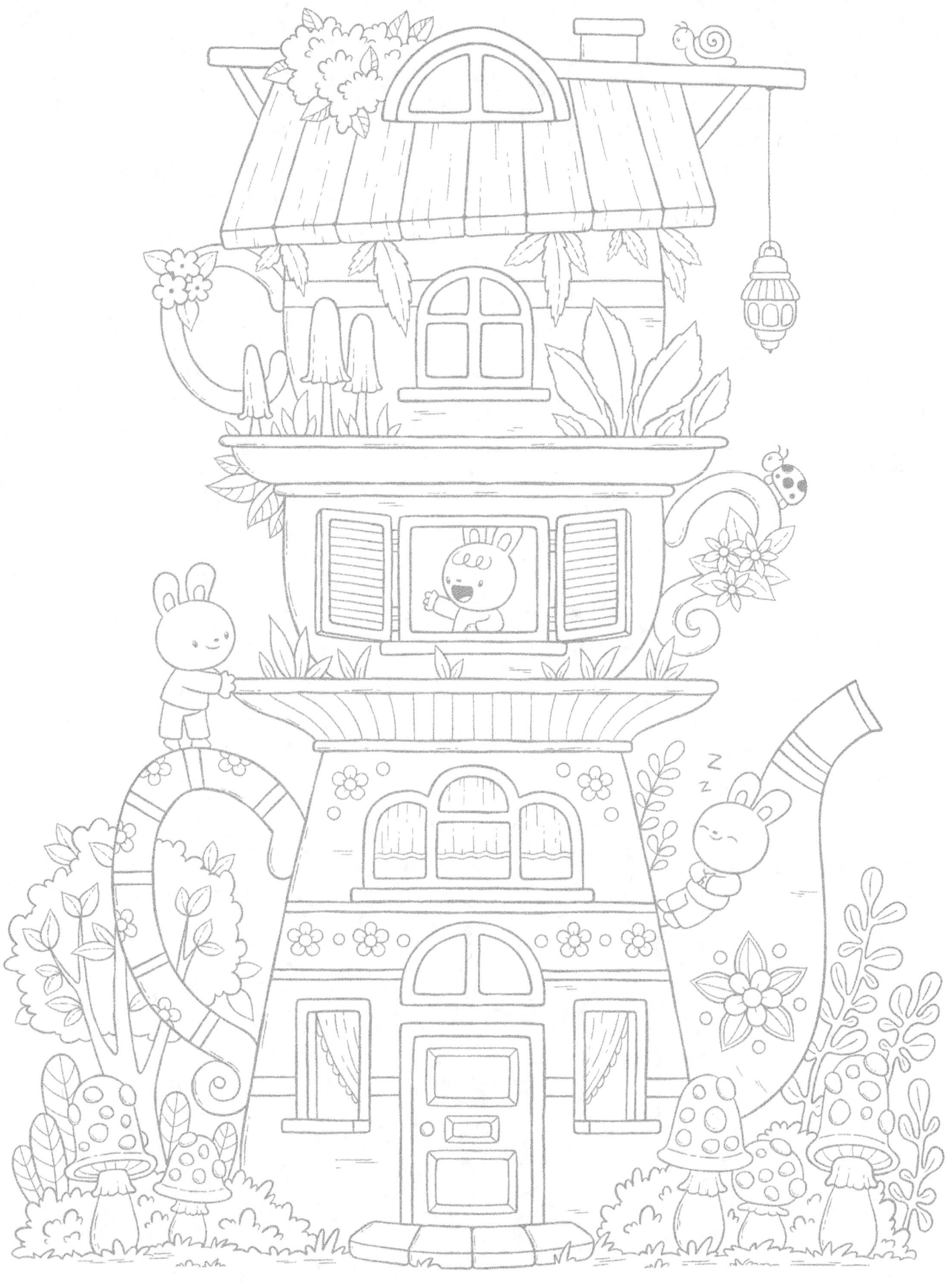

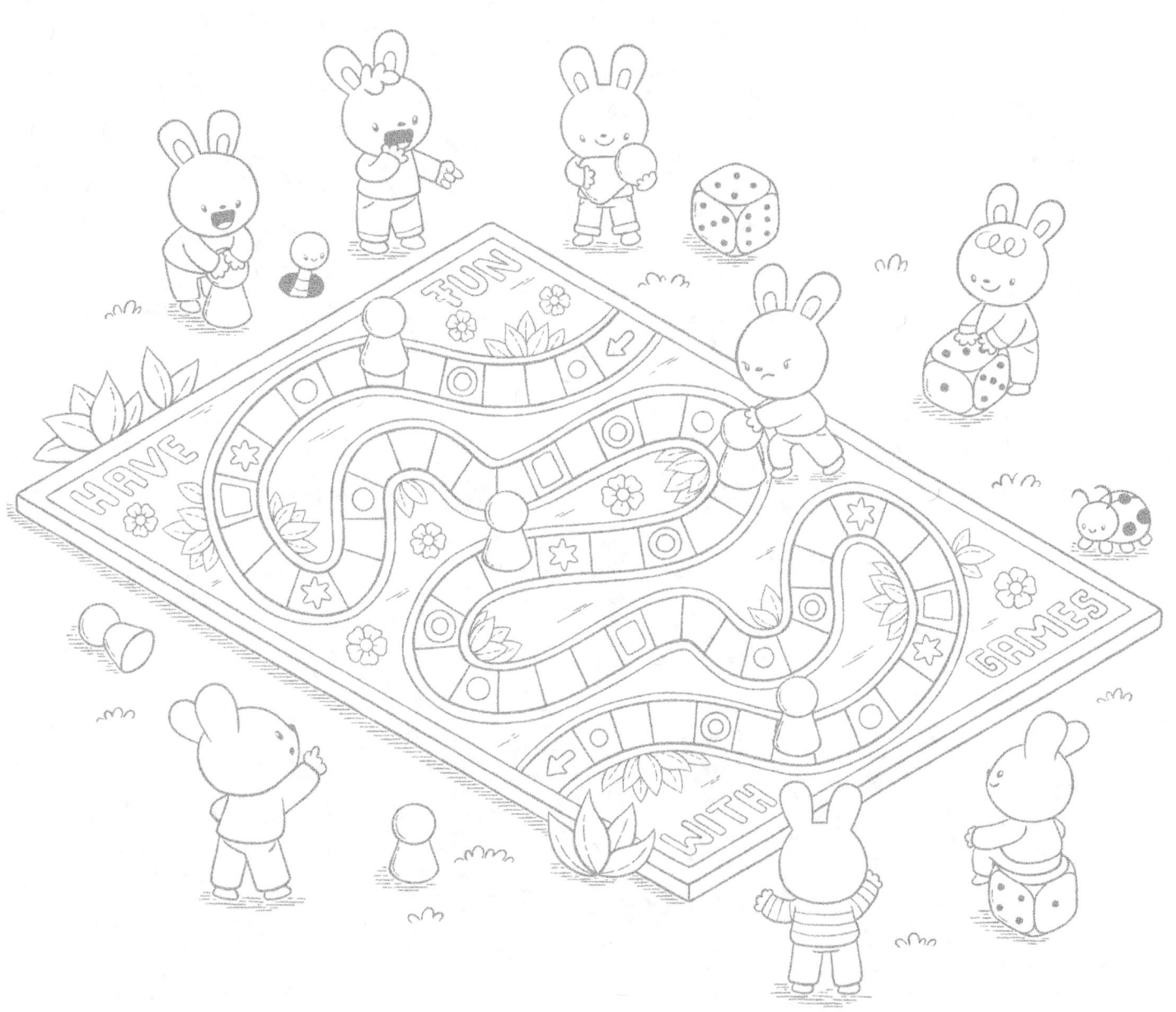

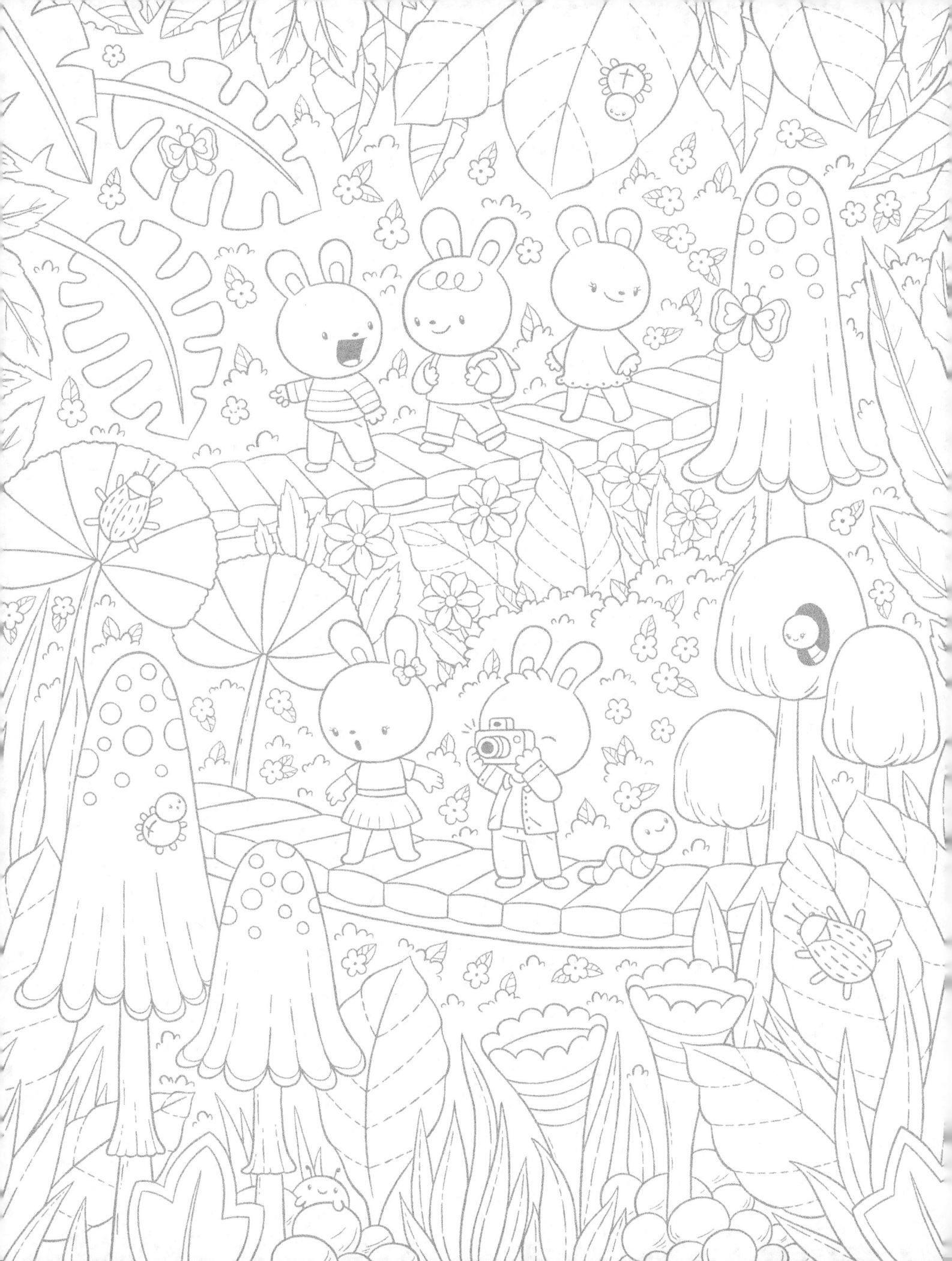

Color Test Page

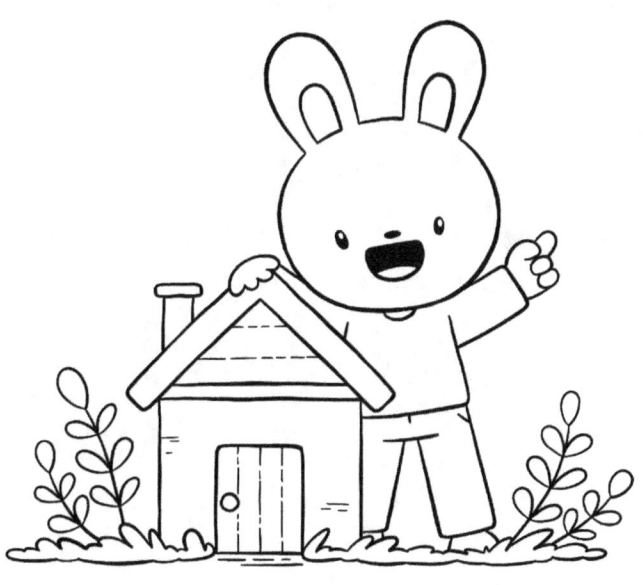

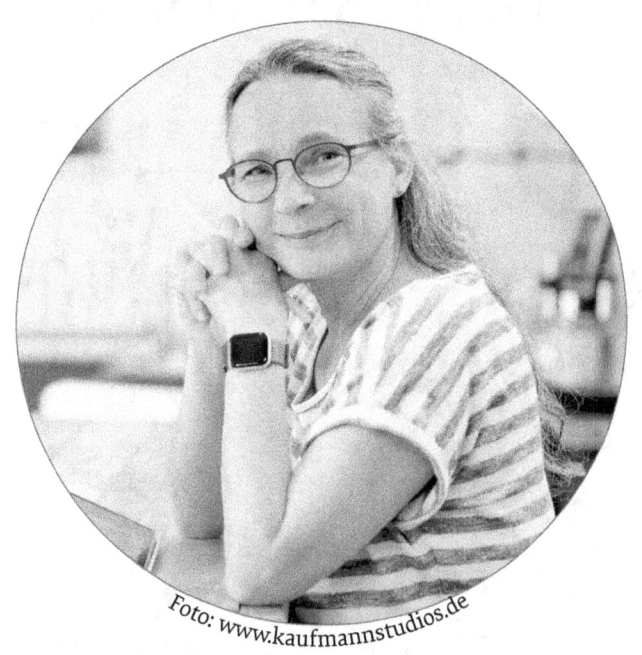

We have now reached the end of the book. I hope you enjoyed the pictures and had a lot of fun coloring them. Pleas have a look at my other coloring books. You can find information about them on the following pages, on my website, on Amazon or on social media.

www.gabiwolf.de
hello@gabiwolf.de

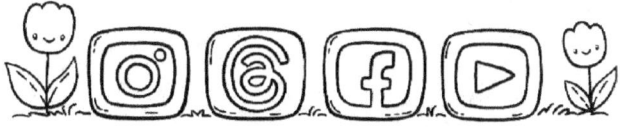

@gabisgrafiken

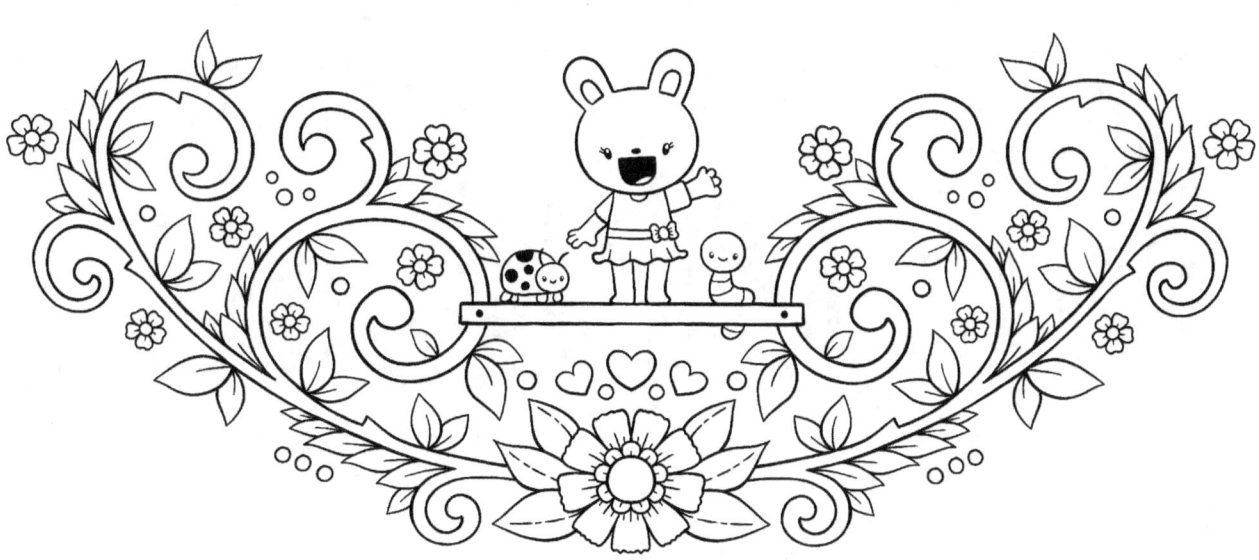

More Coloring Books from Gabi Wolf

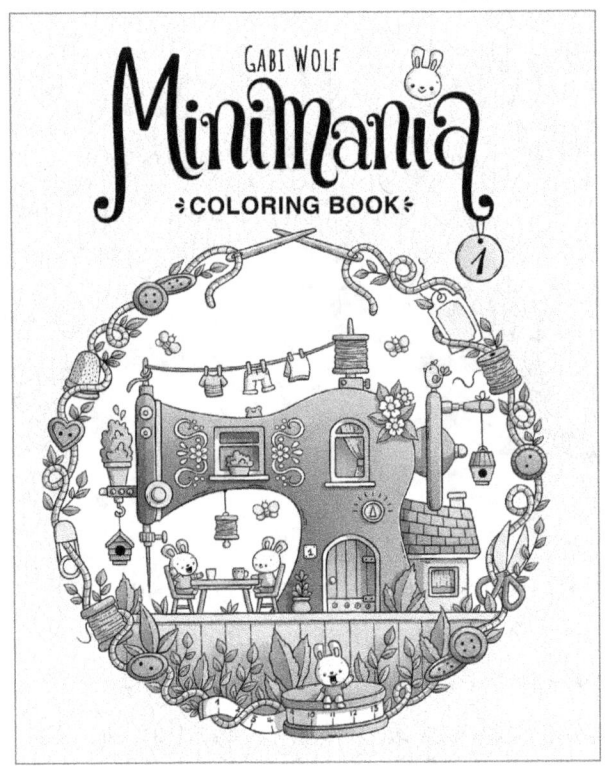

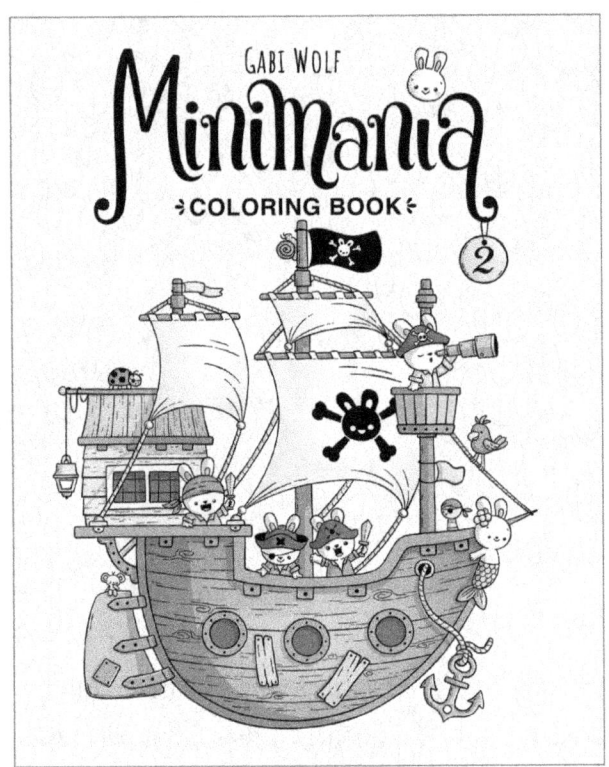

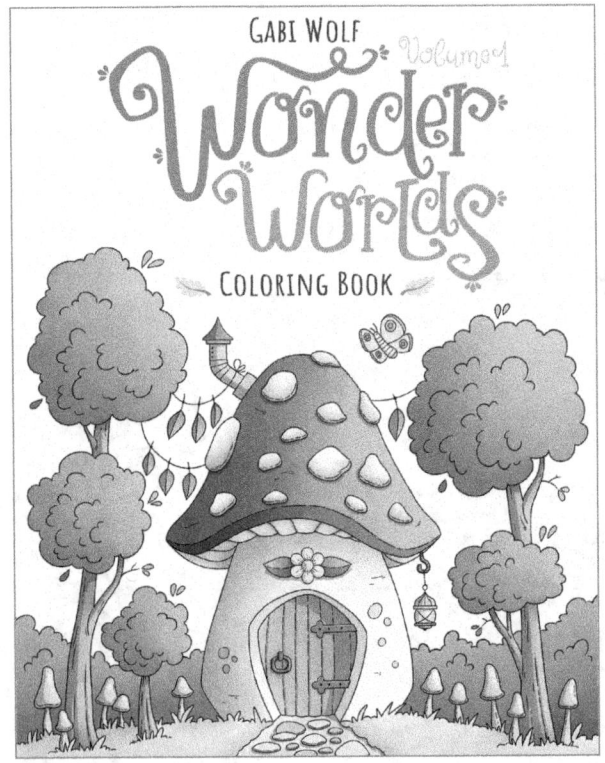

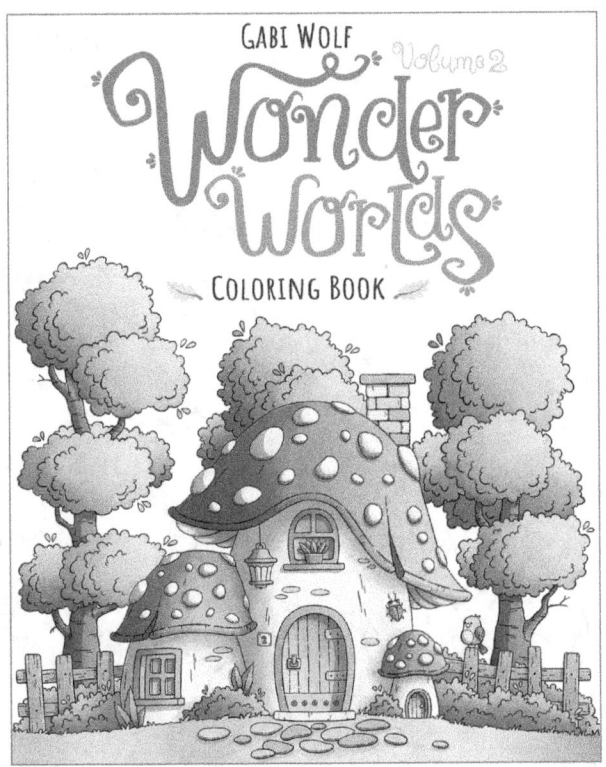

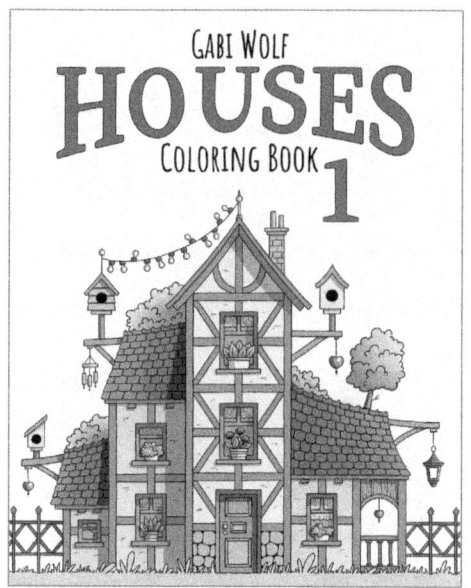

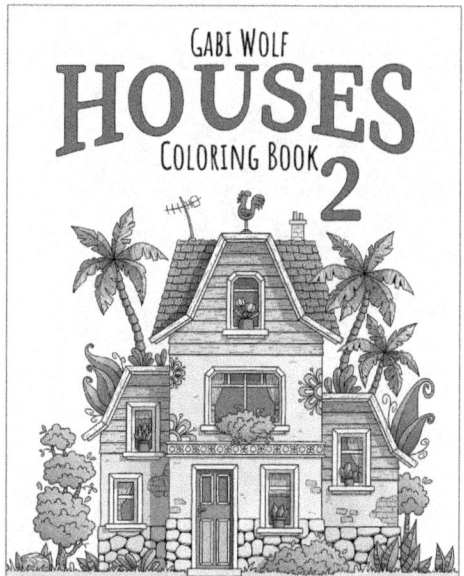

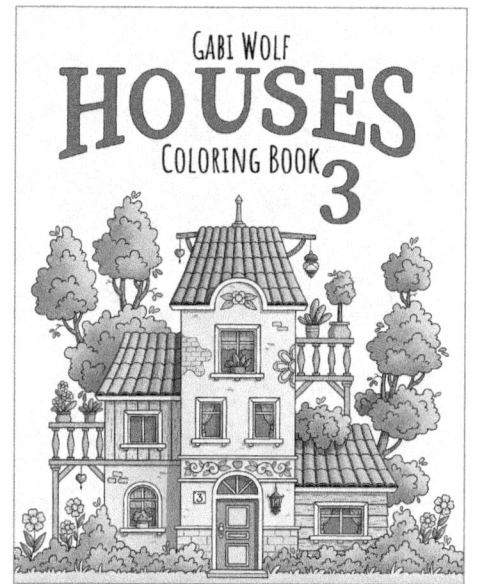

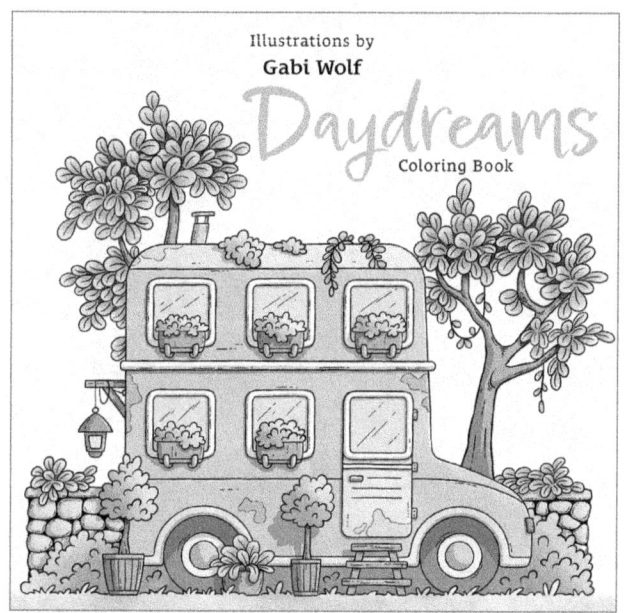

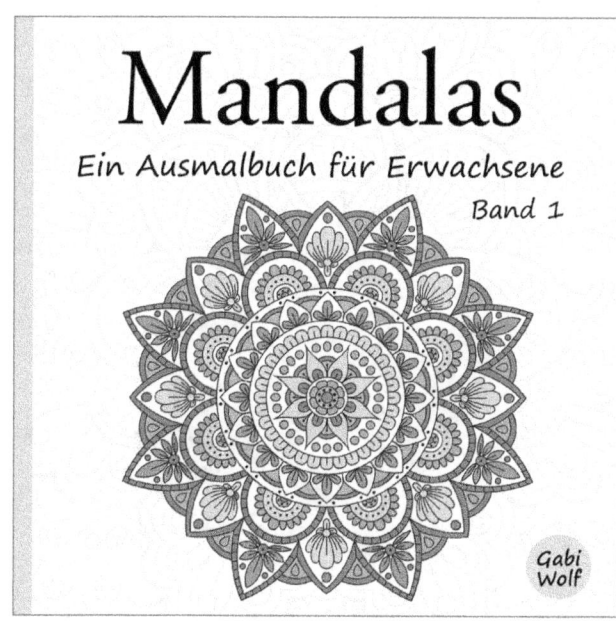

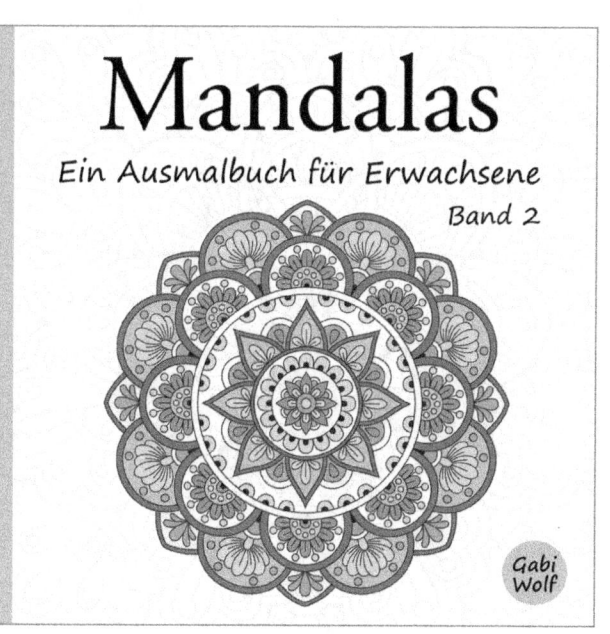